LONDON INTERIORS

LONDON
INTERIORS

FROM THE ARCHIVES OF COUNTRY LIFE

JOHN CORNFORTH

AURUM PRESS

For N.
In memory of O.S.

First published in Great Britain 2000 by Aurum Press Limited
25 Bedford Avenue, London WC1B 3AT

Text copyright © 2000 by John Cornforth
Photographs © by *Country Life* Picture Library

A catalogue record for this book is available from the British Library.

ISBN 1 85410 668 6

Designed by James Campus
Series Editor: Michael Hall

Originated by Colorlito-CST S.r.l., Milan
Printed and bound in Singapore by CS Graphics

Frontispiece: *Staircase at Dorchester House.*
Front endpaper: *Regent Street, early 1920s.*
Rear endpaper: *Belgrave Square, 1924.*

THE COUNTRY LIFE PICTURE LIBRARY

The *Country Life* Picture Library holds a complete set of prints made from its negatives, as well as those from *The King*, and a card index to the subjects, usually recording the name of the photographer and the date of the photographs catalogued, together with a separate index of photographers. It also holds a complete set of *Country Life* and various forms of published indices to the magazine. The Library may be visited by appointment, and prints of any negatives it holds can be supplied by post.

For further information, please contact the Librarian, Camilla Costello, at *Country Life*, King's Reach Tower, Stamford Street, London SE1 9LS (*Tel*: 020 7261 6337).

HOUSES

The following is a list of the primary articles in *Country Life* featuring the principal houses included in this book. In the following key, the name of the photographer is given first (where known), then the date of the article(s), followed by the author.

Westminster
Ashburnham House: A. E. Henson, 2 and 9 December 1933, Lawrence E. Tanner (pair of articles on Westminster School; A. E. Henson, 3 September 1943, Christopher Hussey.
North House: A. E. Henson, 24 June 1933, Christopher Hussey.
Gayfere House: Arthur Gill, 13 February 1932, Christopher Hussey.
Mulberry House: A. E. Henson, 6 June 1931, C. H. Reilly.
15 Queen Anne's Gate: Edward Hudson's house was photographed several times by *Country Life*, but, with the exception of some objects in Hudson's collection, the photographs seem not to have been for publication. Those reproduced here were taken by Sleigh and Ward in about 1920.

St James's
Norfolk House: A. E. Henson, 25 December 1937, Arthur Oswald.
Spencer House: Arthur Gill, 30 October and 6 November 1926, Earl Spencer.

Green Park
Pomfret Castle (18 Arlington Street): A. E. Henson, *Country Life* Annual 1970, pp. 138–9, John Cornforth.
19 Arlington Street: Charles Latham, 1902, *The King*; F. Sleigh, 17 September 1921, Arthur T. Bolton.
22 Arlington Street (Wimborne House): Charles Latham, 1902, *The King.*
Devonshire House: Charles Latham, 1903, *The King*; photographer unknown, 22 August 1914 and 20 September 1919, Arthur T. Bolton.
Flat designed by Oliver Hill in the new Devonshire House: Arthur Gill, 1927, vol. 46, p. 356, C. H. Reilly.

Mayfair
66 Brook Street: Photographer unidentified, 21 April 1928, vol. 63, pp. 558–65, Christopher Hussey.
12 North Audley Street: A. E. Henson, 11 April 1925, Christopher Hussey; Alex Starkey, 15 November 1962, Christopher Hussey.
44 Grosvenor Square: Alex Starkey, 27 July 1961, Reginald Colby.
44 Berkeley Square: A. E. Henson, 8 July 1939, Arthur Oswald; Alex Starkey, 27 December 1962, Mark Girouard.
45 Berkeley Square: Arthur Gill, 2 January 1937, Christopher Hussey.
Lansdowne House: Photographer and author unidentified.
19 Hill Street: (Rex Whistler's mural) photographed for an article by Edith Olivier, 'Memories of Rex Whistler', 1 September 1944.
26 Hill Street: (Rex Whistler's murals) A. E. Henson, 25 March 1939, Christopher Hussey.
75 South Audley Street: Charles Latham, 1902, *The King.*
Chesterfield House: Mr Ward, 25 February 1922 and 4 March 1922, H. Avray Tipping. The library also contains unpublished photographs taken in 1931.
16 Mansfield Street: Arthur Gill, 26 April 1930, Christopher Hussey.

Park Lane
5 Hamilton Place: Charles Latham, 1902, *The King.*
Londonderry House: Charles Latham, 1902, *The King.* A. E. Henson, 10 July 1937, Arthur Oswald.
Dorchester House: S. W. Westley, 5 and 12 May 1928, Christopher Hussey.
Brook House: Original house, Charles Latham, 1902, *The King.* The Mountbattens' penthouse in the block of flats which replaced it was the subject of an article by Christopher Hussey with photographs by A. E. Henson, 24 June 1939.

North of the Park
Portman House: Charles Latham, 1902, *The King.*
Home House (20 Portman Square), subsequently the Courtauld Institute of Art: photographer not known, 15 November 1919, Arthur T. Bolton; A. E. Henson and Arthur Gill, 15 and 22 October 1932, Christopher Hussey.
The following houses were photographed for an article by Christopher Hussey, 'Four Regency Houses', 11 April 1931: 11 Titchfield House by Arthur Gill and 11 Montagu Place by A. E. Henson and Newberry.
The Holme: Mr Thompson, 28 October 1939, G. C. Taylor.
1 Bedford Square: A. E. Henson, 6 February 1932, Christopher Hussey.
90 Gower Street: unpublished photographs by an unidentified photographer.

From Belgravia to Kensington
5 Belgrave Square: A. E. Henson, 26 February 1938, Christopher Hussey.
Kingston House: A. E. Henson, 20 March 1937, Christopher Hussey.
Lowther Lodge: Charles Latham, 1902, *The King.*
180 Queen's Gate: Alex Starkey, 30 August 1956, Christopher Hussey.
Houses in Kensington Palace Gardens were photographed by Jonathan Gibson for two articles by Mark Girouard, 11 and 18 November 1971.
8 Palace Court, Bayswater: Charles Latham, 1902, *The King.*
18 Stafford Terrace: unidentified photographer, 4 April 1952, Christopher Hussey.
West House, Campden Hill: Charles Latham, 1902, *The King.*
Holland House: Charles Latham, 17 June 1905, 'H.B.'.

ACKNOWLEDGEMENTS

It would have been impossible to have done this book without Camilla Costello, who, over the years, has turned the *Country Life* photographic archive from a collection of dusty, collapsing boxes of negatives into an efficient photographic library, and in the process has made many discoveries, not least the negatives from *The King*. Together, Camilla and Olive Waller, who has been involved with *Country Life* almost as long as I have, have devoted many hours to building up mountains of photocopies from prints, looking out negatives and getting them printed up, as well as answering my endless stream of requests for more.

As always, even in a supposedly wordless book, many people have helped me in different ways. Among those to whom I am grateful are David Beevers, Charles Cholmondeley, Adrian FitzGerald, Rupert Lord and Alex Starkey.

CONTENTS

IT is thought odd to prefer London walks to those in the country, but one of the West End's great strengths is that it continues to be so visually and historically stimulating at walking pace. It is always possible to get away from dull or ugly streets such as Oxford Street, or Bond Street, or, even worse, Victoria Street, and concentrate on the historical pattern of streets linking the network of squares that form the centres of many central London estates. These streets are seldom too long or too straight to become boring, and they are still usually subtly paced out by the original plot sizes and resulting bay schemes, with all their variations in size and details of handling – doors with porches and balconies, obelisks and fanlights, windows sometimes swelling out to become bows or bays, and so on. And even when houses are rebuilt, the plot sizes often survive to dictate the rhythm of the street. The squares, particularly those laid out in the seventeenth and eighteenth centuries, are remarkably human and comfortable in scale for walking; and it is only the bigger, more monotonous nineteenth-century squares of Belgravia that would be better viewed from a horse-drawn carriage.

The mixture of materials, their different colours and textures, with the predominance of brick and stucco over Portland stone, also contributes to London's humanity, while the changing aesthetic of recent decades has made enjoyable in a new way juxtapositions of Georgian, Victorian and Edwardian buildings that used to jar, with post-1918 buildings sometimes making welcome contributions. Even Grosvenor Square, as rebuilt in the years after 1930, now seems to be enlivened by the way that its completion has been held up by the survival of the pale-brick Victorian façade of the Italian Embassy on the east side, and the painted stucco façade of No. 38 on the south side. All the time one's reaction to the townscape is changing.

In thinking about materials it is easy to forget the improvement in the atmosphere, particularly in winter, when darkened buildings used to loom out of the fog, and how much cleaner London has become and how much crisper all its buildings look. In the early 1920s *Country Life* published a fascinating, but often forgotten, series of articles on London streets by Professor C. H. Reilly, its architectural editor, and it is striking how dingy and dead most of the buildings, particularly plain Georgian houses, looked compared with their appearance today. This should be remembered when lamenting the extent of the destruction that has gone on in this century.

Night-time walks have a special fascination because of the rewards of seeing richly ornamented ceilings lit up at night by glittering chandeliers. It is always cheering, for instance, to look up at the façade of 44 Berkeley Square and see William Kent's mosaic ceiling glowing with colour and gilding, or to get a glimpse of the seemingly unpublished ceiling at Sackville Street, or the newly restored music room at Home House, Portman Square.

In the past it often used to be possible to wander into former private houses that had changed their uses, such as 8 Clifford Street or 20 Cavendish Square, and ask to have a glimpse of their painted staircases, or to enjoy Spencer House when it was occupied by

Christie's, or Coventry House when it was the St James's Club, or Ely House, Dover Street, when it was the National Book League. But, if one looks prosperous enough, it is still possible to ring the bell of Bourdon House and pretend that one has a house in Chester Square to furnish (because it is the last good house to be used as an antique shop), or call at 39 Brook Street to look at Wyattville's drawing office in Avery Row. In the 1960s and 1970s, it was 'the bed-sit' of Mrs Lancaster, a Virginian by birth who had a profound influence on the look of English interiors after the Second World War through her series of houses and her ownership of Sybil Colefax and John Fowler. That connection enabled her to live here and make it the most glamorous room in London.

Most of these, however, are relatively minor pleasures, because London now has very little to compare with the palaces of Rome or Vienna or the great *hôtels* of Paris, which have survived better because they tend to house extended families in series of apartments – a concept unknown in London. The maintenance of a large London house was usually tied up with the political role of a landed family, while its use was also influenced by the significance of the sporting calendar in the family's life. This kept many families out of London except when Parliament was sitting and the Season was in progress. Thus, when families' political responsibilities declined and the sporting life continued, the costs of a London house seemed unjustifiable. So many of the finest private houses have been demolished in the last eighty years, and of those that survive, none

BERKELEY SQUARE Opposite: *The plane trees in Berkeley Square, seen from the front door of No. 13 in 1937.*

1 GREEK STREET Above: *The entrance to 1 Greek Street, Soho Square. One of the few Georgian houses that can be visited.*

The former Isthmian Club in what had been the Marquess of Hertford's house in Piccadilly in 1922. An illustration from one of the series of articles on London streets written by C. H. Reilly in the 1920s that record many buildings now disappeared.

remain in sole private occupation. On the other hand, the names of streets and squares and buildings tell anyone who is curious a great deal about the history of London and its builders over the past 350 years, and it is the particular combination of the present and echoes of the past that help to make London so enjoyable. Thus, when whirling by in a bus – or more often grinding past – the Dorchester Hotel in Park Lane, it is easy to imagine it away and Robert Holford's Italianate mansion back in position.

What makes such imaginative reconstructions possible are the records of photographers, with two names being particularly important, Bedford Lemere and *Country Life*. Harry Bedford Lemere, who joined his father's photographic business when he was seventeen in 1881, photographed a number of great houses in London before *Country Life*, and indeed many more London interiors. A number of these are reproduced in Nicholas Cooper's

The Opulent Eye (1976), among them views of Chesterfield House and Norfolk House, both taken in 1894, and Dorchester House, taken in 1905. The sets of photographs taken by *Country Life*, starting with Holland House in 1905, tend to be fuller and they provide an invaluable record of a number of houses, sometimes at key moments in their history. Most of these photographs have such a distinctive quality that even when they are reproduced without acknowledgement on the page, they invariably say '*Country Life*'.

On the other hand, it is also striking how many houses *Country Life* did not record: there are no photographs of Montagu House, Whitehall, nor of Lancaster House when it was still in occupation as Stafford House, nor Apsley House before it became a museum.

The *Country Life* collection also contains a number of negatives of London houses dating from the early years of the century. None of them appear to have been used in the magazine, but since some were reproduced in a short-lived weekly paper called *The King* in 1902, they may have been passed on, because that magazine also belonged to Sir George Newnes. It was launched on 6 January 1900 as *The King of Illustrated Papers, a Pictorial Record of the World's News*.

LONDON ELEVATIONS

Top: (left) *19 Grosvenor Square, as it was in 1919, and now demolished;*
(right) *20 St James's Square, as it was in 1917, and subsequently doubled in size.*
Above: (left) *Home House, Portman Square, as it was in 1919, and still there;*
(right) *180 Queen's Gate, as it was in 1956, and demolished in 1971.*

9

However, it did not catch on in that form, and it was revamped in March 1902, with more than a look over its shoulder at *Country Life*, although it concentrated on personalities rather than places. Royal topics were central and photographs of American heiresses in London were part of the diet; and, what is of concern here, it started a series on London houses clearly modelled on what *Country Life* was doing on country houses, no doubt hoping to attract advertising for London property. It began with Londonderry House, but after six months it showed signs of faltering and was abandoned after Devonshire House appeared in March 1903, just before the paper itself was closed. Almost inevitably, many of the glass negatives have disappeared over the years, and so the choice of illustrations here has been confined to those that survive rather than having the volumes in the Cambridge University Library photographed. There are also negatives of London houses not used in *The King* and some of these cannot be identified.

It is not clear whom *The King* used as a photographer, but it was possibly Charles Latham. He took splendid photographs for several architectural books in the late 1890s, and began to work for *Country Life* in 1898. In the opening years of the new century he illustrated the folio volumes of *Gardens Old and New* and *In English Homes* for

Country Life, but his name does not appear in the magazine after 1909, when the third volume of *In English Homes* appeared. Recently a letter has come to light at Arbury Hall that suggests that he and H. Avray Tipping, who by then had became the principal country-house writer, did not get on. Also there is evidence in Tipping's articles on Combe Abbey, which he had rephotographed, although Latham had taken a series of photographs not long before.

It is also worth remembering how patchy has been the coverage of the West End by the Survey of London in its multi-volume record of historic buildings throughout the city that began in 1897. Neither the southern half of Mayfair nor the Arlington Street area has yet been described; elsewhere, its approach has been strictly historical, with only limited illustration of interiors, and furnishings and works of art outside its brief. Nor have there been the equivalent of the various Parisian surveys of areas and periods that have gathered and illustrated a great deal of documentary material, or books as

60 KNIGHTSBRIDGE Above: *The gallery at 60 Knightsbridge. A photograph from* The King *of the house of Lady Naylor-Leyland, who was American and so of particular interest to the magazine.*

SOUTH LODGE, RUTLAND GATE Right: *A photograph from* The King *of Lord Llanggattock's house.*

detailed as Jean-Pierre Babelon's *Demeures Parisiennes sous Henri IV et Louis XIII*, or Michel Gallet's *Paris Domestic Architecture of the Eighteenth Century*.

In its first decade *Country Life* showed little interest in London houses, with Holland House the earliest to be described in 1905, largely because it was a country house in London. The first contributor to concentrate on eighteenth-century London houses was A. T. Bolton, an architect who was curator of Sir John Soane's Museum from 1917 until his death in 1945. He is still remembered for his two monumental volumes on Robert Adam which were held up by the First World War and did not appear until 1922. However, there are signs of his working towards the book in 1913 with a series of short but unusually carefully researched articles on town and country houses. These are usually overlooked because they are rarely included in bound volumes of the magazine, and the earlier ones are also omitted from the index. Today one place where they can be found is in a set of rather battered, bound volumes concentrating on *Lesser Country Houses* kept in the *Country Life* photographic library. Among the London houses described by Bolton are 20 and 32 Soho Square; Stratford Place; Portland Place; 7 and 20 Mansfield Street; 17 Hill Street; 15 St James's Square; Fitzroy Square; and 19 Grosvenor Square.

Bolton's first article was soon followed up with signs of concern in the magazine about the destruction of London, as can be seen over the case of 75 Dean Street, the first test for the Ancient Monuments Consolidation Act of 1913. Efforts to save it eventually failed after the War, when the house was dismantled and the painted staircase was taken off to the Art Institute of Chicago. In 1914 Edward Hudson, personally, and *Country Life* contributed to the Victoria and Albert Museum's acquisition of the Hatton Garden room. Many of the photographs reproduced here were taken for articles that were pleas or obituaries, or records that proved to be obituaries. But behind some of them was a sense that many of the buildings had outlasted the world for which they had been created, and nothing, or at least very little, could be done to hold up progress, whether it meant destruction caused by greedy developers or London University, or, in the case of Grosvenor Square, a desire both to make money and impose a Georgian Revival uniformity on what had always been an architectural muddle. This concern for what was disappearing gathered pace in the mid 1920s, when Christopher Hussey became the architectural driving force. Indeed by the late 1920s, his, and so *Country Life*'s, growing concern about the future of country houses was seconded by another article about the destruction of London. By the 1950s, when he was beginning to think about what became the *Late Georgian* volume of his country-house series, which goes up to 1840, he was starting to write about Victorian houses, such as 18 Stafford Terrace and 180 Queen's Gate, and as late as 1962 he was having to make a strong defence of Nash's Sussex Place in Regent's Park.

However, it is often forgotten how concerned *Country Life* was with new architecture, even if Christopher Hussey had difficulty getting evidence of the modern movement into the magazine in the late 1920s. The most obvious sign of this interest in new work was Edward Hudson's championing of Lutyens, which will hardly emerge here because none of his London houses were major works, as can be seen from their omission from the *Memorial Volumes* produced after his death. However, Lutyens had a very considerable influence on Hudson and so on the character of *Country Life*. Also, he in turn was influenced by what he saw in the magazine. He regularly suggested ideas to Hudson, which probably explains articles such as the one on Rex Whistler's painting on the walls of the staircase in 19 Hill Street, the home of Lutyens's eldest daughter, Barbara. There are also the contributions of Lawrence Weaver, although he did not write about London subjects, and of Professor C. H. Reilly, who wrote about the work of architect friends whom he admired, including Darcy Braddell and Oliver Hill. Oliver Hill indeed came only second to Lutyens in the amount of attention he received over a very long span, but then he became a great friend of Christopher Hussey, and for several years before the latter married,

19 GROSVENOR SQUARE Opposite: *The saloon was designed in 1764 by Robert Adam for the 8th Earl of Thanet, and echoed his design for the saloon at Kedleston.*

Above: *A chimneypiece at 19 Grosvenor Square. London houses must have contributed generously to the international trade in chimneypieces, and most, like this one, have disappeared without trace.*

he shared Hill's weekend house, Valewood. Lord Gerald Wellesley was also a close friend of Hussey, and again Hussey had shared his weekend house, Chips, near High Wycombe, before he went to Valewood. Another architects' practice that owed a great deal to *Country Life* was Seely and Paget, although none of their work is illustrated here. Publication of what they did for Sir Neville Pearson, a director of *Country Life*, and his wife, the actress Gladys Cooper, at 1 and 2 The Grove, Highgate, in 1931, set them off on jobs in Highgate that lasted until Paul Paget finally retired in 1969.

If *Country Life* helped these architects through publication of their work, they would probably have also said how much they owed to *Country Life* as a source of ideas and information, as did both Oliver Hill and Francis Johnson. Thus, when new work is found in the magazine in the years before the Second World War, it is always worth considering how and why it appeared.

*   *   *

When I was asked to make a book of *Country Life* photographs of London houses, the first idea of concentrating on Great Houses had

to be quickly abandoned, because it was impossible to do a photographic equivalent of Beresford Chancellor's *Private Palaces of London* (1908). On the other hand, the magazine has photographed a great many interiors, often in houses that could never be called 'great', particularly original ones of the inter-war period. So it soon became clear that the book should be devoted to domestic interiors and concentrate on those that were recorded in private occupation. This has presented a marvellous opportunity to recapture the scale of *Country Life* between the wars when the page size was larger and there seemed to be no restriction on the length of architectural articles, the number of parts or the size of illustrations, particularly of details; and it soon turned into a much richer feast that I had envisaged. However, that also meant leaving out Royal palaces or

14 QUEEN ANNE'S GATE   Below: *An unpublished* Country Life *photograph, probably taken at the request of Edward Hudson, who lived opposite, of the dining room designed by Samuel Wyatt, where Charles Towneley displayed some of his principal classical marbles.*

CHESTERFIELD HOUSE   Right: *The ballroom on the first floor, which was formed in the 1880s by Lord Burton out of one of Lord Chesterfield's original rooms in the French style and whose decoration he copied in the extension beyond the screen of columns.*

17 HILL STREET *The drawing room as it was in 1917. It was designed by Robert Adam for Sir Abraham Hume, and although only some of the bones of the decoration are seen here, Adam's drawings show that it was one of his most elaborate later London interiors.*

residences, official houses and buildings, institutions and clubs, fascinating as some of the records are. Thus the late Duke and Duchess of Kent's house in Belgrave Square, the Walpolian kitchen of 10 Downing Street, the Foundling Hospital on its original site, and the Astor Estate Office are among those that have had to be omitted.

It also meant deciding how far to go from Westminster without getting caught up in villas and country houses now swallowed up in Greater London, such as Fenton House and Kenwood in Hampstead, Cromwell House on Highgate Hill, Old Battersea House across the river, and Asgill House at Richmond. Quite soon I found that I had to confine myself to an area bounded by Holland House and its estate on the west, by Regent's Park on the north, but with a short diversion to take in Titchfield Terrace, Regent Street on the east and the river on the south. This meant omitting a number of interesting interiors in Soho, Lincoln's Inn Fields and the Adelphi, in particular 1 Greek Street, which has some of the best mid-

eighteenth-century plasterwork in London, and 60 Carey Street, a modest house with slightly earlier plasterwork and decorative painting on the staircase.

At the same time I had to decide how to arrange the pictures: this could be by the date they were taken to record *Country Life*'s own history, or, a better idea, by the date of the building of the house, but the problem with that was that some photographs, such as those of Home House, are more interesting as records of their own time than of the Adam interior, even though they still remain the best set.

So in the end I decided to arrange them as if the reader were being taken on a walk, looking at London interiors through the eyes of *Country Life* mainly between the years 1918 and 1939, but with a few earlier and later pictures as well. It begins in the shadow of Westminster Abbey, and after many twists and turns and hops from period to period, but broadly reflecting the development of central London, it ends up at Holland House. The advantage of such a walk is that it makes it possible to take a reader behind façades that are deliberately discouraging, such as those in Hill Street, Mayfair, and show more than glimpses of ceilings which usually can only be gained at night when rooms are lit up. At the same time, since London buildings tend to keep their old names, however unworthy they are of them today, the sight of those names can bring to mind what used to stand there. The walk also passes many notable façades, which can only be mentioned, and those associated with famous people, as can be seen from the blue plaques that they bear.

The majority of the illustrations have been chosen for their pictorial quality, as a tribute to *Country Life* photographers of the past, but some have been chosen for architectural reasons, while others provide evidence about interior decoration. I particularly wanted to bring out the political and social role of houses and the difference in scale between eighteenth- and nineteenth-century interiors which reflect the surprisingly small-scale, close-knit character of early- and mid-Georgian society, and the more extravagant style in the years after the Battle of Waterloo.

Inevitably there are many photographs that I would like to have included, but, if readers are persistent, most, but not all, can be traced through the Cumulative Index, which includes a section on London Buildings and Places but, infuriatingly, also puts a number of London houses into the main section of Town and Country Houses and Gardens.

Country Life's concern at the destruction of London needs to be seen in a longer view of the city's history: it has never been a static city and it has always been rebuilding itself. As Celia Fiennes

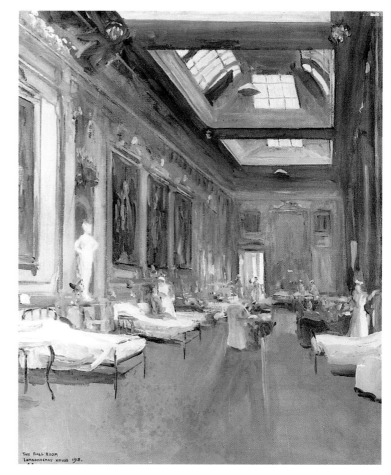

LONDONDERRY HOUSE   *The gallery in use as a hospital ward during the First World War, as painted by Sir John Lavery.*

observed at the beginning of the eighteenth century: 'There were formerly in the City several houses of the noblemens with large gardens and outhouses and great attendances, but of late pulled down and built into streets and squares and called by the names of the noblemen, and this is the practice of almost all even just to the Court excepting just one or two.'

A few years later, Daniel Defoe went into more detail: 'All those Palaces of the Nobility, formerly making a most Beautiful Range of Buildings fronting the Strand, with their Gardens reaching to the Thames, where they had their particular Water-gates and Stairs, one of which remains still, viz. Somerset House, have had the same fate, such as Essex, Norfolk, Salisbury, Worcester, Exeter, Hungerford and York Houses; in the Place of which are now so many noble Streets and beautiful Houses, erected, as are, in themselves, equal to a large City and extend from the Thames to Northumberland House.'

Part of the reason for this constant change has been that London has always been an expensive place in which to live, and it has always taken exceptional means to build and maintain a great house there. Thus even before the Civil War there were noblemen anxious to increase or at least restore their fortunes through development of their houses and gardens. The 4th Earl of Bedford built the piazza in Covent Garden on the site of the garden of Bedford House, and Lord

COUNTRY LIFE

Vol. LXXII.—No. 1871.   SATURDAY, NOVEMBER 26th, 1932.   [Price One Shilling]

THE MARCHIONESS OF LONDONDERRY

The 1932 Country Life *frontispiece of the Marchioness of Londonderry, the wife of the 7th Marquess.*

Southampton petitioned to demolish his house in Holborn 'as his fortune felt need of some help'. In the early eighteenth century Lord Burlington developed part of his garden, and in the nineteenth century parts of the grounds of Kingston House and Holland House were built over.

Very few families were as consistently rich as the Dukes of Devonshire and so able to build and maintain a great house over a long period. Most of the bigger houses were the result of sudden increases in fortunes or large legacies. Lord Chesterfield, for instance, was only able to build his house because he inherited money, as did his wife. Spencer House was made possible through the bequest of Sarah, Duchess of Marlborough, to her favourite grandson. Thomas Anson, a Staffordshire squire, was only able to build 15 St James's Square because he inherited the fortune of his brother, the Admiral. Londonderry House was acquired because Lord Londonderry's second wife was the greatest heiress of her generation, and Dorchester House was built out of the unexpected profits of the New River Company. And this situation continued until 1939, as will be seen with The Holme in Regent's Park, 5 Belgrave Square and 15 Kensington Palace Gardens, all of which were transformed because of exceptional fortunes.

usually three, or sometimes four, bays wide with a simple façade. As James Ralph wrote of such houses in 1734: 'Many a nobleman whose proud seat in the country is adorned with all the riches of architecture, porticoes and columns ... is here content with a simple dwelling, convenient within and unornamented without.'

In 1750 Madame du Bocage wrote with a typical sense of French superiority: 'About a dozen buildings, which are here called Palaces, but at Paris would pass only for large houses, and which men of fortune amongst us would find many faults with, are highly esteemed in London; but there are many large squares, that have something grand in them. To tell the plain truth, though there is great luxury in England, it does not come up to ours, which the people of this country imitate nevertheless, as all the nations of Europe do, to their destruction.'

French influence on English taste in interiors, particularly in London, can be traced in a series of waves from the time of Madame du Bocage down to the years immediately before the Second World War, when Stephane Boudin created a number of striking rooms in London, as can be seen here in the illustrations of 5 Belgrave Square and The Holme. However, that came to an abrupt end in 1939, and at present it is hard to envisage it reviving. Indeed, if someone plots a similar *Country Life* London walk in fifty years' time, there will probably be few more photographs to illustrate the second half of the twentieth century. Yet there have been glamorous, if not great, new rooms in London, particularly by John Fowler for clients such as Mrs David Bruce, the Baroness Philippe de Rothschild and, of course, for his partner, Mrs Lancaster, but usually they were not photographed when fresh, and sometimes not at all; certainly, sadly, never by *Country Life*. So, a future generation will look in vain in its archives for Fowler rooms, or those by Felix Harbord, Geoffrey Bennison and Montgiardino, and only find one room by David Hicks (and that unindexed). And will any rooms by these designers survive intact in London in 2050? Probably not, because while buildings can be saved from demolition by legislation, that does not preserve complete interiors, and they usually only survive as bones, and often sad bones waiting to be brought to life again by old photographs.

Double-page advertisement in Country Life *announcing the demolition sale of Norfolk House in 1938.*

Eighteenth-century society was small and only increased slowly during the first three quarters of the century, as demonstrated by the number of peers. There were 161 in 1704 and still only 182 in 1780. However, in the last sixteen years of the century, 120 new English ones were created, and together with the Irish peers, this brought the number to almost five hundred by the end of the century. In 1790 it cost about £10,000 a year to maintain a country house and a town house with ease, and there were perhaps only four hundred families in that position. It explains why rich families accepted a street house

Opposite: *Pulling Down London. 'How We Celebrate The Coronation', a page from* Country Life, *16 April 1938, with a collage of demolished London buildings that includes a number of houses illustrated here, including Dorchester House, Lansdowne House, Norfolk House, Kingston House and Chesterfield House.*

PULLING DOWN LONDON

A TRACT FOR THE TIMES

OH, a fisherman's life is a life that's gay
    As he sails on the open sea,
And a vagabond's life on the great highway
    Is a life that is fine and free,
The steeplejack and the blacksmith black
    Rejoice in their employment,
But a job I've got that tops the lot
    For open-air enjoyment,
        As here
        I stand
      My pick-axe in my hand,
        'Neath God's
        Blue sky
      I make the plaster fly—

Pulling down London, smashing up the town,
    That is the life for me,
A-breaking up of beauty and a-knocking of
        it down,
    Under the sky so free,
      So whack that roof and bang those walls,
        And scatter the old brickbats,
      And down with the Adelphi, and the
        Temple and St. Paul's,
        And up with the service flats,
          By Gee,
        Yes, up with the service flats.
Sir Christopher Wren was all right then,
    But he ain't no great shakes now,
So drill that drill, my lads, until
    You can't see the dust for row.
Oh, the face of the world is changing fast,
But only fossils want things to last,
So shiver the foundations and blast the past,
      Pulling down London Town.

If aeroplanes with bombs on high
    Destroyed what I destroy,
Oh, wouldn't there be a great outcry,
    You bet there would, my boy.
      If what them Adam Brothers built
        Was bashed by the foe's barrage,
      Oh, wouldn't we shout about the guilt
        Of doing it free of charge,
          By Gee,
        Foreign labour free of charge !
But who will grouse if Pembroke House
    Is bust by an Englishman,
Or shake his fist if I assist,
    At the death of the best Queen Anne.
There's not much money in the past that's gone,
But there's oodles in a bran-new Odeon,
So civilisation marches on,
      Pulling down London town!

HERBERT FARJEON.

ONE

WESTMINSTER

Today, Westminster and Whitehall are thought of in terms of public buildings and monuments, not private houses and domestic interiors,

and it is hard to envisage this area as largely covered by the two Royal palaces that, by the time Whitehall was gutted by fire in 1698,

rambled from the site of the Houses of Parliament to what is now Trafalgar Square. Of the palaces, two great interiors survive:

William Rufus's colossal Westminster Hall, built in the 1090s, with its huge hammerbeam roof made for Richard II by Hugh Herland,

and James I's Banqueting House at Whitehall, designed by Inigo Jones in 1619, with Rubens's ceiling added in the mid 1630s.

Here many Stuart courtiers had their quarters, and later, in the eighteenth and nineteenth centuries, a number of families built fine houses;

but with Montagu House, Pembroke House, Gower House and Harrington House having gone and only Gwydir House and the

former Fetherstonhaugh House surviving, ministry buildings, headed architecturally by the Treasury and the Foreign Office, have won

the day. However, from the west door of Westminster Abbey, the arch into Dean's Yard beckons, and one of the most

atmospheric architectural walks in London begins.

ASHBURNHAM HOUSE

In the shadow of Westminster Abbey, but hidden away in Little Dean's Yard and now part of Westminster School, is one of the most exciting interiors in London: the staircase at Ashburnham House. It is the first of a series of imaginative Classical staircases in London houses which spanned the two centuries from 1660 to 1860, ending with that at Dorchester House (see frontispiece, page 122 and page 123).

Naturally, the Ashburnham House staircase became part of the Inigo Jones legend in the first half of the eighteenth century, particularly after Lord Burlington, Jones's great champion, had designed the neighbouring Dormitory for Westminster School in 1722, but, in fact, the house was probably by John Webb. That was the family tradition passed on to Batty Langley, who wrote in 1736 that it was designed by Webb for William Ashburnham, Charles II's Cofferer of the Household, in the early 1660s.

The approach to the staircase is narrow, but as soon as it comes into view, with the balustrade of another flight climbing upwards, the Ionic pilasters pacing out the upper storey and the hint of an opening to yet another storey above, it is clear that something special is about to happen. But it is only at the foot of what proves to be the third flight that the landing is seen behind its Ionic porch-cum-loggia, with the pilasters becoming columns, and the oval opening in the ceiling, with its balustrade and trios of slim columnets, is fully revealed. And when the landing is reached, there

is the view of the well and the oval above framed by the Ionic order.

The staircase was engraved by Isaac Ware in his *Designs of Inigo Jones* and so surely both Kent and Adam were aware of it when they came to design their staircases at 44 Berkeley Square (pages 79–82) and Home House (pages 140 and 141); later it was greatly admired by John Soane. If the *Country Life* photographs taken by A. E. Henson in 1933 and 1943 – to illustrate articles by Lawrence Tanner and Christopher Hussey – are put together, they show how the staircase is made to look monumental and actually works within a confined area measuring only 23 feet by 14 feet 6 inches. The collaboration of photographers and authors is important in the composition of *Country Life* photographs, because the author invariably chooses the subjects and gives the photographer precise instructions about the angles of view. So when two sets exist, as in

ASHBURNHAM HOUSE, WESTMINSTER   Preceding pages (left): *The house in Little Dean's Yard, with the Victoria Tower of the Palace of Westminster, photographed in 1933. The plain exterior hides one of the most unexpected seventeenth-century interiors in London.*
(right): *The ante-room at the head of the stairs, with boldly detailed woodwork from the early 1660s.*

Above: *The Charles II staircase. When these two 1933 photographs are combined with the one on the right, taken in 1943, they show how the complete design works.*

Right: *The head of the staircase, with the oval opening in the ceiling revealing a false upper storey and dome.*

this case, the second author would have been aware of the earlier set when planning the new pictures and would have wanted fresh compositions, a point that will be illustrated at 44 Berkeley Square.

¶ *From Dean's Yard to Smith Square is one of the best architectural walks in London, making a series of early Georgian doglegs along Barton Street, then into Cowley Street before turning again to have the view of Archer's St John's Church, Smith Square, triumphant at the end of Lord North Street. This starts at the crossing with Great Peter Street, and on the right-hand corner stands a remarkable double house which echoes some of the details of its earlier and humbler neighbours, even if it does tower over them – Oliver Hill's North House and Gayfere House.*

NORTH HOUSE AND GAYFERE HOUSE

Country Life has become so associated with the recording of historic buildings that it is usually forgotten that before the Second World War, it published a great deal of new domestic architecture and architectural decoration, and in the late 1920s and early 1930s, the magazine promoted a modern style growing out of the Classical tradition. This became a particular mission of Christopher

Hussey's and so helps to explain why so many of Oliver Hill's commissions were illustrated in *Country Life* from 1921 to 1969. As Alan Powers wrote in 1989: 'Oliver Hill has long been recognised as a quintessential figure of the inter-war period, a dabbler in many styles, and a brilliant architectural decorator.' But the difficulty for posterity is how to approach his modern work, because modernists of his own time, whose social and intellectual ideas he did not share, did not regard him as one of themselves. However, as Alan Powers wrote in his conclusion: 'Now that the myth of an undivided modern movement has been universally acknowledged as a myth, Hill's passionate divided loyalty must be recognised as part of a cultural problem which has been ignored for too long ... He may have come closer to a synthesis than we can easily recognise.'

The problem of how to assess him is apparent in these two houses where the interiors are in quite different styles to their

GAYFERE HOUSE, WESTMINSTER Above: *The drawing room, with walls of green-silvered mirror glass and silver-grey oak. The Lutyensesque house was by Oliver Hill, with modern interiors designed in collaboration with the client, Lady Mount Temple.*

Right: *The mirrored bathroom, which Lady Mount Temple told Oliver Hill showed her from forty-seven different angles.*

exteriors. Also, they are a reminder that there was still a real difference between a London style and country style. In fact, the whole scheme involved four houses, with the larger North House, on the corner of Wood and Lord North Streets, being built for Mr Robert Hudson MP, its promoter, while Gayfere House next to it belonged to Lord and Lady Mount Temple. Mr Hudson (1886–1957) entered Parliament in 1924, and was married to Hannah Randolph, from Philadelphia. In 1940, he became a highly effective Minister of Agriculture and was made a Viscount in 1952. Lord Mount Temple had inherited Broadlands in Hampshire and was the father of Lady Louis Mountbatten by his first marriage to the elder daughter of Sir Ernest Cassel (see Brook House); after her death in 1914, he married the Hon. Mrs Forbes-Semphill.

NORTH HOUSE, WESTMINSTER Left: *A mirrored bathroom designed for Mr and Mrs Robert Hudson by Oliver Hill and published in* Country Life *in 1933, at the time of the Exhibition of British Industrial Art.*

Above: *The honey-coloured marble staircase, with verdigris bronze window grilles and balustrade.*

Externally, the building displays Oliver Hill's life-long admiration both for Lutyens and for Norman Shaw's 170 Queen's Gate, which so impressed him as a boy; but at the same time it is subtly different from both, being lighter in spirit and handling.

The principal interest of Gayfere House, which was illustrated first, lay in the elaborate treatment of the drawing room and the main bedroom and bathroom which were designed by Lady Mount Temple in collaboration with Oliver Hill. The drawing room was a fusion of the new and the Baroque, with walls of glass backed with small squares of green silver foil and pilasters, and panels of silver-grey oak which disguised the jib doors. These also formed shutters at night that folded over the windows, while the chimneypiece and overmantel of eighteenth-century inspiration were carried out in engraved looking glass. Silver became a leitmotif for the decade, as will be frequently seen. Oliver Hill was fascinated by the possibilities offered by the new ways in which glass was produced. Moreover, he had a painter's eye as well as an architect's, which enabled him to respond to a very wide range of objects and

materials, both hard and soft, man-made and natural, and he was always able to draw on his vivid historical memories and imagination. Thus he was a brilliant architectural decorator.

The choice, arrangement and positioning of flowers also played a significant role in the decoration of the room; this must have been considered new at the time, because the two vases of real flowers and the arrangement of artificial ones, 'in a composition reminiscent of Van Huysum or Baptiste', are mentioned in the article as being by Flower Decorations. That was Constance Spry's first shop, near Victoria Station, which she opened in 1929, five years before she brought out her first book, *Flower Decoration*.

Christopher Hussey described the idea of the bedroom as being 'the cool green of deep water: a bed set in a crystal alcove and resting on crystal feet, standing on a milk-white floor. The walls and ceiling are glazed green. The bed-cover and chair of zebra-skin.' Earlier he wrote: 'The ideas are, in large degree, Lady Mount Temple's, Mr Hill interpreting them into form. Both parties were free to criticise and protest, though each undertook not to destroy anything original in the work of the other.' It is hard to believe that all went smoothly with the job or that Oliver Hill behaved like a proverbial lamb, because he invariably used every trick in the book to get his own way.

He particularly enjoyed designing stylish bathrooms, a new craze from America in the 1920s, and encouraged fashionable people to commission what were sometimes the only modern rooms in their houses. An alternative was to treat them as attractive additions to bedrooms and dressing rooms, like Lady Diana Cooper (page 155) with carpets, curtains, wallpapers, and pictures. But he seldom got the chance to design a *cabinet des glaces*, with walls and ceiling in grey mirror, a black marble floor, and a bath of gold mosaic with blue glass vessels in sky-blue recesses, and blue towels.

North House was published in June 1933, at the time of the Exhibition of British Industrial Art at Dorland Hall, which was chaired by Christopher Hussey, had Oliver Hill as exhibition architect, and was supported by *Country Life*. On its General Committee were Robert Hudson, Lady Mount Temple and Lady Melchett, as well as Professor Reilly. Hussey took North House as a demonstration of the aims of the exhibition to promote 'the middle course in contemporary English design' and 'a solid and intelligible modern style'.

Being a larger house, more space could be devoted to its entrance and staircase hall, where a short flight led up from the front door to the main level with its pair of simplified Ionic columns, and to the first flight of the staircase, the whole apparently influenced by Oliver Hill's visit to the Stockholm exhibition in 1930. The staircase was of honey-coloured Ciampo Perla marble inlaid with green verditer; this related to the verdigris bronze of the balustrade,

MULBERRY HOUSE, SMITH SQUARE *The drawing room by Darcy Braddell, with its overmantel relief of* Scandal *by C. S. Jagger and wall paintings by Glyn Philpot, depicting* The Loves of Jupiter *against a New York background, as illustrated in 1931.*

whose own pattern was reflected in the grilles to the blind windows which provided artificial light. Such play with light was another novel feature of interior design at the time.

Again, he pulled out all the stops in the principal bathroom. It had an oval bath lined with silver mosaic and was set against grey mirror glass. And he thoroughly enjoyed getting a magazine to agree to publish a photograph, supplied by him, of this bathroom complete with naked models.

¶ *Smith Square is usually thought of as being a completely Georgian enclave because of its north side and the church, but, in fact, the north-west side is a twentieth-century version of that, with Lutyens's Mulberry House of 1911 on the corner of Dean Trench Street, and next to it Venice Yard House and 12 Gayfere Street, both designed by Oliver Hill in 1923.*

MULBERRY HOUSE, 36 SMITH SQUARE

Seventy years on, such elaborate and imaginative architectural interiors as those in North House and Gayfere House seem to belong to a remote world, and so it is fascinating to be able to make a local comparison round the corner at Mulberry House. In 1930 it was acquired by the Hon. Henry Mond, soon to be the 2nd Lord Melchett, and his wife, and it was for them that the dining room and drawing room were remodelled by Darcy Braddell. The articles were published in 1931 by Braddell's friend, Professor C. H. Reilly. Initially, Braddell worked with the sculptor, C. S. Jagger, and then in the drawing room with the painter, Glyn Philpot, as well. Reilly described the drawing room as 'one of the boldest, most complete and original schemes of decoration of our time'.

15 QUEEN ANNE'S GATE Above: *The dining room of Edward Hudson, the founder of* Country Life. *Here many of the ideas for the magazine were developed over lunch.*

Right: *The drawing room. The detail in both these rooms appears to be by Edwin Lutyens, who altered the house for Edward Hudson, one of his most consistent patrons and promoters.*

Sadly the article does not explain how the commission came about, merely saying that the alterations were carried out for Lady Melchett, which is not the complete story. Braddell's connection with the Monds went back to 1911, when he had altered Melchett Court, near Romsey, for the 1st Lord Melchett after it was first acquired by him. By the time the house was illustrated in *Country Life* in 1930, the gardens contained notable modern sculpture, in particular two fountains by C. S. Jagger. Braddell, working with H. Deane, had also just completed a new modern house on the estate, Woodfalls, for the Henry Monds. Thus the Smith Square commission can be seen as growing out of the Mond family tradition of patronage and collecting, with Woodfalls and Mulberry House taking it forward into the modern age.

The visual emphasis of Reilly's article is on the drawing room, but Philpot's involvement may have been suggested by Mrs Mond after work began. After sitting to him for her portrait – one of the successes of the Summer Exhibition at the Royal Academy in 1927 – she became one of his principal supporters.

Originally it seems the room was intended to be closer in spirit to the dining room. The photographs of that room (not taken by *Country Life*) are not quite as successful, and so it is difficult to visualise the effect of its polished travertine walls, designed as a stripped Classical setting for Greek antique marbles and vases, but Professor Reilly wrote of how 'one feels on entering that here is some fine, cool, rather noble room of a Roman patrician'.

Turning to the drawing room, he continued: 'The room as Mr Darcy Braddell designed it was simple, light and bright, with silver foil walls, green bronze doors with polished cream marble architraves, the treatment of the chimneypiece wall with its overmantel relief of *Scandal* by Jagger being worked out by the architect and sculptor together. After Mr Braddell and Mr Jagger came Mr Glyn Philpot's painted decoration, depicting on the silver foil in a series of half-magical drawings *The Loves of Jupiter*, painted in transparent colours of grey, black, pale blue and pink, and totally unexpected in his oeuvre at this date ... The neo-cubist treatment of a New York skyline may reflect a similar scheme which Philpot may have seen in America, but its use as a background for his mythologies helps to create an atmosphere of urban sophistication appropriate to the room.' The room was destroyed in the war and all that survives is Jagger's relief.

¶ *From Smith Square it is natural to be drawn down Dean Stanley Street to catch a glimpse of Lambeth Palace across the Thames, and walk north along Millbank. Ahead lie the cupolas and domes of Whitehall, but now that Montagu House, Pembroke House and Gower House have all gone, leaving only Gwydir House and the former Fetherstonhaugh, later York House and now the Scottish Office, there is little of a domestic character to pull one in that direction. So the walk cuts between the Abbey and St Margaret's Church and then heads across Broad Sanctuary to Old Queen Street, which leads into Queen Anne's Gate.*

15 QUEEN ANNE'S GATE

It is revealing of the taste of Edward Hudson, the founder of *Country Life*, that he chose to live in an early-eighteenth-century house in Queen Anne's Gate that looked back to the late seventeenth century and the Age of Wren. The house was a perfect foil to the much grander 'Wrennaissance' building in Covent Garden that he had commissioned in 1904 from his hero, Edwin Lutyens, as the office for *Country Life*.

Hudson had started the magazine in 1897, partly to make better use of his family printing and blockmaking business, and had gone into the then new business of illustrated magazines with Sir George Newnes, but he had always been fascinated by old houses. So, from the start, he made an article on a house *Country Life*'s central feature. However, he had not yet established the magazine's style of writing or photography when he met the thirty-year-old Lutyens with, or through, Gertrude Jekyll in 1899, and gave him his first commission to design Deanery Garden at Sonning, in Berkshire.

The first article on Lutyens's work appeared in *Country Life* the following year, and Hudson also started to recommend him to people who sought his advice. The restoration and conversion of Lindisfarne Castle, Northumberland, followed in 1903. The alteration of his own London house came after that. Lutyens evidently opened up the small rooms, giving them new cornices, panelling and chimneypieces. He may also have designed the bed in Edward Hudson's bedroom.

The understated character of the house, both externally and internally, suited the furniture and objects. Hudson liked the way that he arranged them, with a strong sense of pattern, such as the group of small pictures and ceramics over the fireplace in the bedroom. His aim was to create a sense of calm and order and perhaps that explains why here, and in his other houses, he avoided pictures that provided challenges – unlike his commission of Augustus John's portrait of Suggia, the cellist, with whom he was infatuated – but collected prints and coloured prints on glass.

In this he was not alone: it is striking that several of his contemporaries who were more ambitious collectors of English furniture, such as Colonel Mulliner and Percival Griffiths, also seem to have been relatively uninterested in pictures. It was if they were deliberately elevating fine pieces of English furniture to being works of art in their own right and part of the national achievement, rather than being just part of the unity of a room. This remained a strong strain in English collecting until after the Second World War.

The photograph of the dining room is evocative for *Country Life* because it was here that many of the ideas for the magazine were developed over lunch, particularly after Hudson persuaded Lutyens to move his office to the next-door house in 1910, and so could become a frequent guest. Presumably Lutyens designed the apse for the sideboard and the chimneypiece and overmantel, both framed in marble, in a free working of an idea from about 1700, while the oval-back armchair to the right of it was also either

15 QUEEN ANNE'S GATE *Edward Hudson's bedroom. The bed was adapted by Lutyens from the one in Carpaccio's* The Dream of St Ursula.

designed by him or was the inspiration for the set that he designed for the *Country Life* office.

Hudson is such an elusive personality that it is hard to get any sense of how Lutyens regarded him. Clearly *Country Life* and Hudson's support were enormously important to his success, and he must have valued the magazine for the way he could promote an approach to architecture through it and influence the amount and character of the new work published in it between the wars.

¶ *From Queen Anne's Gate the route crosses the bridge over the lake in St James's Park, from which there are views both of Buckingham Palace and Whitehall. Then it goes through Marlborough Gate, past St James's Palace and the Queen's Chapel, and the surprisingly tucked-away entrance to Marlborough House, which was caused by Sir Robert Walpole spiking Sarah, Duchess of Marlborough's intention to have an axial entrance from Pall Mall. Pall Mall is now a street of nineteenth-century clubs and only the façade of Schomberg House, with its caryatid porch, is a reminder of its late-seventeenth- and eighteenth-century character. A little way beyond it, two short streets lead up to St James's Square.*

TWO

ST JAMES'S

The planning of St James's Square in the mid 1660s by the 1st Earl of St Albans marked the start of the development of the West End as the fashionable area close to the Court at St James's Palace. It was to proceed on the system of selling plots for building on long leases, but the original idea of having only three or four large plots on each side to provide 'houses fitt for ye dwellings of Noblemen and other Persons of Quality ...' could not be made to work. So the number of plots had to be increased to twenty-two.

None of the original houses survive, and the square owes its character to its first rebuilding, which began early in the second quarter of the eighteenth century and has left it still representing two centuries of British urban architecture. No. 4 is now the earliest of the bigger houses, built in 1726–28 by Edward Shepherd, who was so active on the Grosvenor Estate. It leads on to houses by Henry Flitcroft, Matthew Brettingham, James Stuart, Robert Adam, C. R. Cockerell and Edwin Lutyens.

What is also striking about the square is how long certain families remained there. No. 5, for instance, was acquired by the 1st Earl of Strafford in 1711, and was owned by his descendants until after 1960. The Herveys arrived even earlier at No. 6, in 1677, and remained there until the 5th Marquess of Bristol sold the house in 1955. The Dukes of Norfolk acquired part of what became Norfolk House in 1722 and continued to live there until 1938, when it was demolished.

NORFOLK HOUSE *Preceding pages (left): The staircase, with exuberant plasterwork designed by G. B. Borra, a Piedmontese architect who worked in London in the early 1750s and decorated the main rooms in the house. (right): The sober entrance hall, with Howard crests incorporated in the frieze, designed by the architect Matthew Brettingham for the 9th Duke of Norfolk. The photographs were taken as a record shortly before the demolition of the house in 1938.*

Above: The music room. The ceiling and most of the French-inspired wall decorations by Borra for the Francophile Duchess of Norfolk are now in the Victoria and Albert Museum.

NORFOLK HOUSE

'Would any foreigner, beholding an insipid length of wall broken into regular rows of windows, in St James's square, even figure from thence the residence of the first Duke of England?' So wrote the anonymous author of *Critical Observations on the Buildings and Improvements of London* in 1771 of Matthew Brettingham's nine-bay brick elevation of Norfolk House on the east side of the square. The house had been begun in 1748 by the 9th Duke of Norfolk, and, when its interior was finally completed in 1756, it was regarded as one of the wonders of London.

A young man who went to the opening of the Grand Apartment described how there were no less than 'eleven rooms Open, three below, the rest above ...' and the 'immense Grandure of the Furniture is scarce to be conceiv'd. Every one alow'd it infinitely superior to any thing in this Kindom ...'. The Duchess sat in the music room 'the whole night that she might speak to every one as they came in', while the Duke was in the Great Room. And 'there was a vast Croud, and a great blase of Diamonds, Lady Granby's

*Rococo decorations in gilded plaster set within the beams of Brettingham's ceiling
in the music room. The plasterwork was done in 1755 by Thomas Clark,
under the direction of Borra.*

were I think the Finest, Lady Rockingham had none on at all, which was not Civil, as every one endeavour'd to make themselves Fine'. Lord Rockingham observed: 'Oh, there was all the company afraid of the Duchess, and the Duke afraid of all the company.'

It always used to be a puzzle how Brettingham, a sound but unoriginal Palladian architect, should have designed such a dazzling series of rooms. Then in 1973 it was discovered that much of their decoration was by Giovanni Battista Borra, a Piedmontese architect; he had gone as draughtsman with Robert Wood to Palmyra and Baalbec in 1750–51, and then accompanied him to London in 1751 to produce the plates for Wood's two books on those sites, published in 1753 and 1757. In 1755, towards the end of his time in London, he was called in to decorate the principal rooms at Norfolk House to satisfy the French taste of the Duchess. Soon after that, he went back to Turin, where he decorated Palazzo Racconigi, in which some of the motifs found at Norfolk House reappear.

NORFOLK HOUSE Left: *The pier glasses and tables in the saloon continued the style of the music room.*

Above: *The nineteenth-century saloon was formed out of the original Green Damask and Red Velvet Drawing Rooms.*

What must have always come as a surprise was the simplicity of the hall, but then Isaac Ware wrote in his *Complete Body of Architecture* in 1756: 'In town a hall is a place of reception for servants, therefore, in this, neither magnitude nor elegance are needful: in the country, where there are other ways into the house, the hall may be an elegant one.' It may also be a surprise to see the porter's hooded chair still there, presumably no longer occupied.

The hall led through to a central staircase with a fine balustrade and rich plasterwork incorporating unusually bold trophies, so providing a foretaste of the splendours ahead on the first floor, while its placing enabled the main rooms to be arranged in a complete circuit, at that time a novelty in London.

The circuit started with an ante-room on the north side of the house, and that led into the music room, which together with the Green Damask and Red Velvet Drawing Rooms, filled the whole of the front on to the square. A special room for music seems to have been a new fashion of the 1740s and 1750s, as is seen here and slightly earlier at Chesterfield House (see page 104). This room, now the most important English interior in the Victoria and Albert Museum, is a combination of Brettingham and Borra, with the former presumably being responsible for the design of the beamed

ceiling, dado and window treatment, and Borra adding the chimneypiece, panelling, and pier and overmantel glasses with their branches for candles. The carving is of an unusually high order and is by John Cuenot, a little-known craftsman, who was either French or of French descent. The Rococo plaster trophies on the ceiling by Thomas Clark are also of superb quality.

In the two drawing rooms, the Classical design of the ceilings is more of a problem, because although that in the first room was also used by Brettingham a little later in the chapel at Holkham, both could be based on plates by Borra. The pier and overmantel glasses and pier tables in the first room are in the same spirit as the glasses in the music room. In the early nineteenth century, the two rooms were joined together to form a large saloon.

NORFOLK HOUSE Left: *The monkey doors in the ballroom were inspired by the monkeys in the French tapestries which originally hung in the room.*

Above: *The ballroom. In the early nineteenth century it received additional decoration and looking glasses, but part of the detail goes back to its original use as a Tapestry Drawing Room.*

Behind the second drawing room was the Great Room with the monkey doors, which reflected details in the original French tapestries ordered for the room. Later, in the nineteenth century, it was turned into a white and gold ballroom, with looking glass. The circuit ended with a state bedroom and state dressing room.

The formation of both a saloon and a ballroom recalls a major change in the pattern of social life in London in the years after Waterloo, as Lady Susan O'Brien explained: 'wheras balls were few in number in 1760, they were very numerous in 1818 ...' and 'the size is not thought of much consequence, as if it is not quite crowded it is not thought good or agreable; more people can be contained in a large one, but the crowd must be equal'.

¶ *From St James's Square the walk continues along King Street, and then crosses St James's Street to St James's Place. There, at the end, Spencer House faces Denys Lasdun's handsome block of flats, 6 St James's Place, in one of the most striking contrasts of style in London.*

SPENCER HOUSE

The timelessness *Country Life* sought in its photographs of interiors came partly from the practical desire to be able to go on using them again in books, but it can be misleading, giving arrangements of houses a false sense of permanence. This applies to the photographs of Spencer House published in 1926. The assumption might be that they show the appearance of the rooms from soon after the 7th Earl Spencer inherited in 1922 at the age of thirty, up to the outbreak of the Second World War, and his removal of many of the fittings in 1941 to save them from possible bombing. In fact, Lord Spencer was only able to live in the house for less than two years, from 1924 until 1926, because he, like his predecessors since 1886, found it too expensive.

With the aid of Turner Lord and Co., he carried out an interesting restoration that represents his generation's rediscovery of eighteenth-century architecture. Afterwards, he was determined to retain the freehold, accepting the ups and downs of tenants. He always kept an eye on the house and liked to show around those who were interested, but it could be to their embarrassment and

SPENCER HOUSE   Left: *One of the most imaginative of all eighteenth-century English interiors – the Palm Room, designed by John Vardy.*

Top: *The dome and apses.*

Above: *View of the Palm Room showing the dome and the complete design of the south wall.*

the alarm of the secretaries working there. However, he also provided vivid glimpses into a vanished age, such as his family's sense of shock when they were given keys to the door because a porter would no longer be permanently sitting in the hall, and the impossibility of having tea on summer afternoons on the terrace because of the smuts getting in the butter. A man of scholarly, if pernickety inclinations, who, if born in different circumstances, would have been very happy in the Victoria and Albert Museum, he was deeply knowledgeable about everything that related to his forebears and his inheritance. He was one of the very few owners who was permitted to write about his own house in *Country Life*, producing four articles in 1926.

In 1768, when the house was newly completed, Arthur Young wrote: 'I do not apprehend there is a house in Europe for its size better worth the view of the curious in architecture, and the fitting up and furnishing great houses, than Lord Spencer's in St James's Place.' That Lord Spencer had been able to embark on it was due to his father having been the favourite grandson of Sarah, Duchess of Marlborough, and his own long minority. As soon as he came of age in 1755, he married Georgiana Poyntz and acquired the site as well as his first architect, John Vardy, the most gifted of Kent's followers.

Building began in the spring of 1756, and Vardy planned the ground floor with a sequence of four rooms beyond the Doric entrance hall, a rectangle with curved corners. First there was a small dining room with a deep apse, then a small drawing room on the corner, and beyond that, overlooking the park, the Great Eating Room with two screens of Ionic columns. Finally, guests came to the drawing room or Palm Room, which Vardy made into one of the most imaginative of all eighteenth-century English interiors. Corinthian half-columns rise from palm trees on its south wall to support a frieze copied from an engraving of that on the Temple of Antoninus and Faustina in Rome; side niches frame the central arch into the domed extension – a central square with three apses and the palm-tree columns repeated, their sprouting branches of leaves filling the pendentives beneath the dome.

However, in 1758, General George Gray, Spencer's architectural mentor, introduced him to James Stuart, who was just establishing himself as a promoter of the new Greek style, and in 1759 he produced a finished design for the Painted Room, which was one of the early landmarks of Neo-Classicism. It is an exceedingly complex design that appears to celebrate the Spencers' marriage

through parallels in mythology, with the panels between the pilasters built up into compositions incorporating smaller, gilt-framed paintings supported by grotesque ornament, and with garlands of flowers in the frieze between the capitals. A pair of candelabra stand between the windows, and the sofas, with their winged-lion arms, are all part of the scheme.

Stuart also designed the adjoining Great Room, over the dining room, one of the most splendid rooms in London with its deep-coved ceiling and its combination of large reliefs (originally and now once again bronzed) and supporters with sprays of leaves and garlands of flowers and vases in the corners, painted in white with green and lavish gilding. He was also responsible for the chimneypiece, with its frieze after the Chroragic Monument of Lysicrates in Athens, and the facing tables and glasses, of which part of one table can just be glimpsed on the right. Thus the house provides a fascinating insight into the rapid changes of taste in the late 1750s that were partly stimulated by the return of William Chambers in 1755 and Robert Adam in 1757–58.

Apart from alterations by Henry Holland for the 2nd Earl, remarkably little was done to the house or its furnishings after that, as can be seen from Bedford Lemere's photographs of about 1895. A comparison of those with the 1926 *Country Life* set shows how the 7th Earl rearranged the original furniture in an orderly, formal way that only regained currency after the Victoria and Albert Museum rearranged Osterley Park in the late 1960s. On the other hand, he was not sympathetic to the weighty splendour of the 1st Earl's taste in Italian history pictures. That is particularly apparent in the Great Room, where he removed, rather than renewed, the damask hangings and replaced them with false panels of painted plaster; moreover, he took out the huge pictures by Reni, Sacchi, Guercino and Salvator Rosa which his ancestor had made such efforts to acquire, but were then out of fashion. Thus he upset the original balance and point of the room as a great picture room, as it was understood in the 1760s, giving it a lighter, thinner look in accord with attitudes current in the early 1920s.

SPENCER HOUSE Above: *The entrance hall.*

Right: *The Great Room, designed by James Stuart in 1759, but with the 7th Earl Spencer's panelling of the walls and choice of pictures. The photographs illustrated the articles written in 1926 by him – one of the very few owners permitted to write about their own house in* Country Life.

SPENCER HOUSE

Top: *Part of the ceiling of the Painted Room.*

Above: *The Painted Room, designed by James Stuart
in 1759.*

46

SPENCER HOUSE *The entrance and chimneypiece walls of the Painted Room – one of the earliest Neo-Classical rooms in Europe.*

It is interesting to compare this with what he did later at Althorp, where, in the 1950s, when it was clear that the family would never return to Spencer House, he installed as many as possible of its fittings as well as its pictures and furniture, as Joseph Friedman describes in his study of *Spencer House* (the most recent and comprehensive account of the house). Also, he was influenced by the enthusiasms of a younger generation of cognoscenti, so that he became more sympathetic to the taste in pictures of the 2nd Earl of Sunderland, who founded the collection in the second half of the seventeenth century, and of the 1st Earl Spencer.

After a long period of hard life in the years after the Second World War, the house was given an immensely thorough restoration by the Jacob Rothschild Group, mainly between 1987 and 1989. A most remarkable project in many ways, it would never have got off the ground, let alone been completed, without the personal commitment of Jacob Rothschild. Not only was it tackled by a public company and so had to be financially viable, but it was technically complicated because it combined preservation and restoration of all the principal rooms with adaptation of the secondary areas for office use. In addition, there was the challenge of restoring the fabric, which involved copying all the fittings that had been removed by Lord Spencer and built into Althorp. The amount of carving was enormous and included the copying of all the original marble chimneypieces as well as some of the furniture. Finally, there came the problem of furnishing the rooms, getting back on loan from the Victoria and Albert Museum the contents of the Painted Room and making good, as far as possible, the loss of the seicento pictures subsequently sold or retained at Althorp. Now, the principal rooms have developed a new commercial social life, but there are more dark suits and fewer blazes of diamonds than in its builder's day.

THREE

GREEN PARK

Close to Spencer House, a subway runs into the park, and then, quite unexpectedly, one of the most impressive trios of domestic buildings in London appears: first, Lasdun's 6 St James's Place of 1958, then Spencer House, and just beyond it Barry Bridgwater House, built in 1846–51. Further south lies Lancaster House, and to the north, the bows and bays of the few remaining houses entered from Arlington Street.

Across Piccadilly, there used to be an answering parade of houses, begun at the Restoration of Charles II with the short-lived Clarendon House, which stood on the line of what became Albemarle Street, facing down the hill to St James's Palace, and continued westwards towards Hyde Park Corner first with Berkeley, later Devonshire, House, and then the three survivors: Egremont House, Coventry House and, finally, Apsley House.

Together, the two stretches formed a noble, if erratic, parade of houses facing Green Park, and it is extraordinary that, as late as 1902, from the Arlington Street houses facing the park: 'You hear the gentle bleating of sheep ... and the far-off hum of traffic in Piccadilly ... sounds no more loudly than might the murmur of the sea.' Then, with several of the houses still occupied by political families, it was still possible to see why Horace Walpole had called it 'the ministerial street'. He was born in the house that Sir Robert had lived in from 1716 to 1732, and is now swallowed up in the Ritz Hotel, and later inherited No. 5, to which his father returned in 1742 and he kept until 1779. Today the street is a mess, whose former character can only be revived through old photographs.

18 ARLINGTON STREET

This must have been the most unlikely house built in London in the mid eighteenth century. Certainly it is the only recorded Gothick one: the fantastic creation of the Countess of Pomfret during her widowhood. The fullest photographic record of it is that made by A. E. Henson in July 1934, shortly before it was demolished.

The only exterior view, taken from the street, shows how the 'keep', looking like a Staffordshire pottery ornament, was set back at the end of a court with a three-storey gatehouse which had been heightened since originally built. Next to it appears the entrance to No. 19 Arlington Street.

18 ARLINGTON STREET Preceding pages (left): *The Perpendicular Revival panelling on the staircase of the only mid-eighteenth-century Gothic Revival house in London.*
(right): *The main house and gatehouse and the entrance to No. 19 Arlington Street, shortly before the demolition of No. 18 in 1934.*

Left: *Detail of the ceiling decoration.*

Above: *One of the rooms commissioned by the Countess of Pomfret, a favourite butt of Horace Walpole, who lived opposite and may have been jealous of the Perpendicular correctness of the detail in her rooms.*

Lady Pomfret, the widow of the 1st Earl who died in 1753, was a favourite butt of Horace Walpole who lived opposite to her, but she is rightly remembered in Oxford: it was she who saved the remaining Arundel Marbles at Easton Neston, which she bought from her son and gave to the University in 1755, where they are now to be seen in the Ashmolean Museum. Most of her contemporaries found her rather a bore and her pretension to learning rather tiresome, but since she had been a Lady of the Bedchamber to Queen Caroline, who surrounded herself with intelligent women, that may have been unfair. Among her close friends was Lady Isabella Finch, the builder of 44 Berkeley Square.

Recently, John Harris has discovered that the house was built by Stiff Leadbetter working in collaboration with Richard Biggs, Clerk of the Works at Windsor Castle from 1745 to 1776. How that collaboration came about is not clear, but Biggs had years of experience of looking after St George's Chapel. That is presumably the explanation for the correctness of the Perpendicular detail of Lady Pomfret's house, which moved beyond the half-digested manner of Batty Langley and Sanderson Miller and the Rococo fantasies of Richard Bentley, and, no doubt to Walpole's chagrin, was earlier than his fan-vaulted gallery at Strawberry Hill. Building began in 1757, and Lady Pomfret was able to walk through its rooms the following year. Presumably the house was not long finished when she died in 1761.

Of the original furniture, the only recorded piece is the Gothick library table at Temple Newsam.

19 ARLINGTON STREET

This house is probably most widely remembered as being the setting for Zoffany's conversation piece of *Sir Lawrence Dundas and his Grandson* in the Library and for its remodelling in 1763–66 by Robert Adam, his first important commission for a private house in London.

It is not clear when the house was built by Lord Cartaret, who succeeded to the earldom of Granville in 1744. He is recorded as living there from 1714 to 1731 and from 1739 to 1760, but from 1732 to 1738, the house was empty. That fits with Lady Cartaret telling Mrs Delany in 1732 that she had 'bought the ground her

19 ARLINGTON STREET Left: *A 1931 view of the vaulted corridor linking the hall and staircase.*

Above: *The front door to Lord Cartaret's house of the late 1730s.*

house stood on in Arlington Street, and my Lord designs to build there'. So, presumably it was the new house that Lord Cartaret occupied from 1739. He had a successful career as a diplomat and politician, although after 1730, he refused to hold any office under Sir Robert Walpole and became one of his leading opponents. But he did not look after his affairs, and after his death his furniture and plate had to be sold and this house disposed of to Sir Lawrence Dundas.

The *Country Life* photographs taken in 1921 do not make it clear how the house worked. Nor is it known who designed it. The site, like that of No. 18, was unusually deep, and the Arlington Street entrance was in the centre of a single-storey range with a mansard roof. That seems to have led from a hall through a deep, vaulted corridor with strong pilasters and bold doorcases into the top-lit staircase hall off which opened the main rooms.

Robert Adam redecorated the upper parts of the staircase hall, adding a set of four large allegorical canvases in *grisaille* by Cipriani to the walls at first-floor level, with plaster panels of grotesque ornament and a screen of Ionic columns above. However, he did not alter the decoration of the two first-floor drawing rooms, which retained their original ceilings of the late 1730s. Sir Lawrence made both rooms into picture rooms hung with crimson damask, and for the first, the Great Room looking eastwards, Adam designed and Chippendale made the famous set of seat furniture consisting of four sofas and eight armchairs. It was the only known occasion on which Adam and Chippendale collaborated on a set of seat furniture, and Adam's design in antique taste was deliberately intended to complement the earlier decoration of the room.

A generation later, after the sale of Moor Park in 1784, Sir Lawrence's son brought the set of Boucher-Neilson tapestries woven for the gallery there and their related furniture, and installed them in the Great Room. However, it looks as if extra ornament and gilding were added to the room in the nineteenth century.

Chippendale also provided a second set of seat furniture for the long room, later called the saloon, and that was still in the room when it was photographed for *The King* in 1902. On the main wall can be seen *Shipping Becalmed* by Jan van der Capelle, which appears over the chimneypiece in Zoffany's picture and is now in the National Museum of Wales.

When the house was illustrated in *The King* in 1902, it was described as 'in many ways an ideal house for a peer of the realm constantly occupied with public and private affairs, and for a great lady busied with the doings of the fashionable world'. It remained the Zetland town house until the 1930s.

22 ARLINGTON STREET

Before 1914, *Country Life* photographed surprisingly few London houses, but its collection of London negatives is made much more interesting by the survival of those taken for *The King* in 1902. However, by then the *Country Life* style of photography of interiors had been established by Charles Latham, and it seems very unlikely that Edward Hudson would have ever considered using photographs like those of Wimborne House – even if they had come to him at no cost.

The house was originally begun in the early 1740s by Henry Pelham, to the design of William Kent, and then extended and altered by a succession of owners, including the 7th Duke of

Beaufort in 1840 and the 11th Duke of Hamilton in the mid 1850s. It was acquired by the future 1st Lord Wimborne in 1871.

The Wimbornes owed their exceptional fortune to John Guest, who established the Dowlais Ironworks in South Wales. His nephew, John Josiah, was made a baronet in 1838, ten years before he established the family at Canford Manor in Dorset. He married as his second wife Lady Charlotte Bertie, who is more widely remembered as a passionate collector and by her second husband's name, Schreiber. It was their eldest son, Ivor, who bought the Arlington Street house. In 1868 he had married the eldest daughter of the 7th Duke of Marlborough, and the sister of Lord Randolph Churchill. In the 1880s they enlarged and embellished the house,

19 ARLINGTON STREET   Above: *Decoration by Robert Adam and paintings by G. B. Cipriani on the staircase added by Sir Lawrence Dundas in the 1760s.*

Right: *The original Great Drawing Room of the 1730s house, with Gobelins tapestries and related seat furniture by Robert Adam, brought from Sir Lawrence Dundas's gallery at Moor Park, Hertfordshire, in the late 1780s.*

adding, soon after the creation of the peerage, a huge ballroom designed and built by George Trollope and Sons; they also enriched, and so disguised, Kent's Great Room and redecorated the White Drawing Room in the French style. The result was a huge house that could never have hung together satisfactorily because of the plan and changes of style within, as can be seen in *A House in Town*, published in 1984 by Batsford for Eagle Star Holdings.

According to Beresford Chancellor's description of 1908, 'Indeed all the rooms at Wimborne House are essentially living rooms, so that the splendour of their decorations is, as it seems to me, enhanced by the fact that they are made homely by more or less consistent use.' That must explain the deliberately informal mixture of furniture in the ballroom that the camera found so difficult to sort out – and the next generation was to react against.

The 1st Baron's son, who was made a peer in his own right in 1910, four years before he succeeded his father, had very different taste. This can be seen in his approach to Ashby St Ledgers, a Northamptonshire manor house which he acquired in 1902, and greatly extended in an organic, English way with the help of Lutyens between 1904 and 1938, as a deliberate contrast to the Victorian Canford Manor, which he sold in the early 1920s. Also, he remodelled the interior of Wimborne House towards the end of the First World War with the aid of Thornton Smith, architectural decorators based in Soho.

In *Laughter in the Next Room*, Osbert Sitwell gave vivid portraits of both Lord and Lady Wimborne, who was a daughter of Lord Ebury, and of the house, particularly at the time of the ending of the General Strike in 1926. Indeed, it is one of the best expositions of the political role of a host and hostess in a great London house, albeit just before all that finally came to an end at the outbreak of the Second World War in 1939, shortly after the death of Lord Wimborne.

Of Lady Wimborne he wrote: 'Her great beauty, subtle and full of glamour though it was, and the fact that she was the wife of one of the richest men in England, were apt to blind people equally to her political intelligence, interest and experience. The attitude she presented to the world of a fashionable beauty who dressed with daring and loved admiration, the guise of an accomplished woman of the world, which was hers, naturally, by birth, tradition and upbringing, hid from the crowd the clever woman who inhabited this exquisite shell.'

Of the house he wrote: 'it remained a social institution, and in its hospitable rooms could be met many sorts of people, the heads of foreign states, many members of the cosmopolitan world of fashion, and the most prominent men of the three political parties in England, writers, editors and Trade Union leaders. In addition, this mansion, in the middle of the old aristocratic quarter of

19 ARLINGTON STREET *The saloon in 1902, photographed for* The King *with Dundas pictures and furniture, including* Shipping Becalmed, *Adam pedestals from Moor Park, and Chippendale seat furniture designed for the room.*

London, possessed its own older political traditions, to help the conduct of negotiations: for its roots lay in the heart of one of the greatest and of the earliest of British industrial centres. In South Wales, the great Guest Steel Works had for well over a century been ruled absolutely in succession by the head of the family.'

Lady Wimborne was particularly interested in music, instituting a series of subscription concerts in 1932. They are commemorated in Lavery's painting of *Chamber Music at Wimborne House*, exhibited at the Royal Academy in 1937, the most evocative record of grand London house life at the time.

After the War, when the house was put up for sale, it did not find any immediate takers, but late in 1947, it was bought by the Eagle Star Insurance Company, almost certainly with a view to redeveloping the site. In the end the company decided to use it for its West End offices. In 1957 and 1958, however, planning schemes

were submitted for demolition and rebuilding, but at the second stage the building was listed, partly because of the discovery of Kent's involvement; by 1962, after the loss of Londonderry House, attitudes in London at least were changing and it became clear that permission would not be forthcoming.

Twelve years later Eagle Star produced a new scheme that involved restoration of the original double house facing the park and rebuilding virtually everything else on the site. Work on that began in 1977, and so Eagle Star House now presents a new front on to Arlington Street, with a glimpse of the restored façade of

22 ARLINGTON STREET Above: *Painted decoration in the corridor for the 7th Duke of Beaufort in the 1840s, photographed for* The King *in 1902.*

Right: *A 1902 photograph for* The King *of the Louis XVI Revival White Drawing Room formed by the 1st Viscount Wimborne as part of the embellishment of the house in the 1880s.*

Pelham House behind. The treatment of the surviving interiors was a challenging job, particularly in the Great Room, which involved the removal of Thornton Smith's Renaissance scheme and giving back to the room a Kentian chimneypiece – possibly designed by Flitcroft – and new overmantel, doors with doorcases, and dado. Thus once more it appears as nearly as possible as Pelham's house.

DEVONSHIRE HOUSE

Few people today would be able to say where Devonshire House used to stand in Piccadilly, not associating its name with the New York-style block of flats built on its site in the mid 1920s, or with the piers and gates now on the other side of the road, providing an entrance into Green Park. They were brought to Piccadilly in 1838 by the 6th Duke of Devonshire to form a new entrance in the forbidding wall that sheltered his house from those who passed by. The huge eleven-bay house, only the second major building by William Kent and begun in 1733, was austere almost to the point of grimness, particularly after the balance of brick walls and stone dressings was spoilt by their discoloration and the glazing by the 6th Duke's enthusiasm for plate glass.

The siting and form of the house, with an exceptionally wide plot that provided space for a forecourt, followed that of other post-Restoration houses built along Piccadilly. Indeed, Kent's Devonshire House, built for the 3rd Duke, replaced the original house built for the 1st Lord Berkeley, which had been bought by the 1st Duke in 1698 and then burned down in 1731.

The architectural point of the house lay not in its elevations but in its plan, which was much admired, and its decoration as a background for the finest collection of pictures in any London house of its time. The plan was that of a country house in town, with a lower, pillared hall for everyday use, as at Houghton and Nostell Priory, and, for special occasions, a double flight of steps leading up to a two-storey hall in the centre of the house. There were three drawing rooms on the north side of the house and, unusually, a dining room as part of the main run of rooms, with a large library filling most of one end of the house.

22 ARLINGTON STREET Above: *The ballroom, designed and built by George Trollope and Sons for the 1st Viscount Wimborne.*

Right: *William Kent's Great Room of the late 1740s, disguised by the 1st Viscount Wimborne's decoration of the 1880s.*

Both rooms were recent developments, with the Marble Parlour at Houghton, probably first planned by Gibbs but completed and decorated in the early 1730s by Kent, being one of the earliest to survive. The formalising of the dining room, particularly in London, was probably related to the fashion for silver dinner services complete with épergnes, which became established at about that time.

The conception was, in fact, the opposite of that of Norfolk House, begun twenty-five years later, but again, as with that house, the plan was altered in the nineteenth century, first early in the 6th Duke's time when the hall became the saloon, and later, in 1843, when Decimus Burton built a portico to shelter the lower hall, which then became the main entrance, and also the curving staircase with a crystal balustrade leading up from it on the north side of the house. That lay beyond the original Great Drawing Room, which was then joined to the West Drawing Room to form a large ballroom. The Craces were also much involved from 1840, and in 1844, J. G. Crace painted the saloon ceiling in a Neo-Baroque manner.

Looking at the photographs taken for *The King* in 1903 and for *Country Life* in 1914, it is not at all easy to work out what had happened to the rooms in the course of the previous 180 years, but the main impression is of the Kent interiors of the 1730s being greatly embellished by the 6th Duke. However, there was also some work done for the 5th Duke and Duchess Georgiana, with the Red Drawing Room appearing to have been redecorated by James Wyatt. The 6th Duke was an early admirer of Kent's work and not only acquired Kentian pieces at the Wanstead sale and had others made up in a Kentian style, but, like George IV in later years, he could not resist adding extra carved ornaments to frames and panelling, and painted decoration to ceilings as well as over-gilding almost everything in sight.

What the photographs only hint at is the quality of the pictures, and here it has to be remembered that while Chatsworth and Hardwick were expressions of family history and dignity in the eighteenth century, they were not the settings for the ducal collections; it was Devonshire House that was the focus of the family's public, social and private lives. Thus it was natural that the 2nd Duke, a leading figure among the first generation of English collectors in the early eighteenth century, and the most important in the family, who bought many of the pictures as well as the Old Master drawings and prints, the gems and coins and much of the library, should have wanted his possessions in London. So while Thomas Martyn, the author of *The English Connoisseur*, wrote of Chatsworth in 1766 that it 'has very little in it that can attract the eye of the Connoisseur', he could write of the collection at Devonshire House that it 'was surpassed by very few at home or abroad'.

22 ARLINGTON STREET *The northward enfilade from the Great Room to the White Drawing Room.*

In recent years, much has been written about the 5th Duke and his Duchess, Georgiana, and of their son, the Bachelor Duke. In the latter's early days, the house became a much happier place, and Prince Puckler-Muskau wrote of London in 1826: 'The technical part of social life – the arrangements for physical comfort and entertainment – is well understood here. The most distinguished specimen of this is the house of the Duke of [Devonshire], a king of fashion and elegance. Very few persons of rank have what we, on the Continent, call a palace, in London. Their palaces, their luxury and their grandeur, are to be seen in the country. The Duke of Devonshire is an exception – his palace in town displays great taste and richness, and a numerous collection of works of art. The company is always the most select; and though here, as everywhere, too numerous, is rendered less oppressive by the number of rooms: still it is too much like a crowd at a fair. The concerts at D House, particularly, are very fine entertainments, where only the very first talent to be found in the metropolis is engaged, and where perfect order combined with boundless profusion reigns throughout.'

The last period of social brilliance for the house was in the time of the 8th Duke (1891–1908), who before he succeeded had been a leading Liberal politician and was offered the premiership no less than three times. He was not at all interested in social life, and so it is ironical that his period is now particularly associated with the celebrated historical costume ball given on 2 July 1897, two weeks after Queen Victoria's Diamond Jubilee, by his wife, the so-called Double Duchess. Born Louisa von Alten, she married first the Duke of Manchester, but for thirty years was the mistress of the Duke of Devonshire, whom she eventually married in 1892, two years after the death of her first husband. The fame of the ball lives on in contemporary descriptions and through the album of photographs of the guests in their costumes given to the Duchess afterwards by her friends, and revived in *The Duchess of Devonshire's Ball* by Sophia Murphy. The Duchess was dressed as Zenobia, Queen of Palmyra, by Worth, and the Duke as the Emperor Charles V after Titian.

The Duchess of Marlborough remembered: 'The ball lasted to the early hours of morning, and the sun was rising as I walked through Green Park, where we then lived. On the grass lay the dregs of humanity. Human beings too dispirited or sunk to find work or favour, they sprawled in sudden stupor, pitiful representatives of the submerged tenth. In my billowing period dress [she went as the wife of the French Ambassador to the Court of Catherine the Great], I must have seemed to them a vision of wealth and youth, and I thought soberly that they must hate me. But they only looked, and some even had a compliment to enliven my progress.'

DEVONSHIRE HOUSE *The 6th Duke of Devonshire's ballroom, formed from two of the 2nd Duke's drawing rooms, designed by William Kent in the 1730s. At the far end can be seen Jacob Jordaens's* Portrait of Govaert van Surpele and his Wife, *now in the National Gallery, London.*

In 1914 Devonshire House was closed, and it was not reopened afterwards because the 9th Duke was Governor-General of Canada. It was sold in 1920, but there was always a hope that some of its interiors might be re-erected, and so many photographs were taken to show how fittings related to each other; then they were dismantled and put into storage at Chatsworth.

Shortly afterwards heart-rending photographs were taken of the house being demolished. In his autobiography, Professor C. H. Reilly tells how through Edward Hudson of *Country Life* he had met J. B. Stevenson, the managing director of Holland, Hannen and Cubitt and purchaser of the house, who told him: 'We think the right thing to do is to build an American apartment house upon it, costing about two millions. It is very important we should get the right American architect for the job. You, I believe, know them all.' And Reilly goes on to explain how he recommended Hastings of the New York firm of Carrere and Hastings and how he himself became involved with the project.

In 1927 Reilly wrote in *Country Life* about a flat in the new Devonshire House that Oliver Hill had designed for Mr Albert Levy, and surely there is no more telling way of illustrating the

changes of those years than the contrast between the interiors of the two Devonshire Houses. Reilly argued, not wholly convincingly in view of his later article on the decorations at Mulberry House, that one of the differences between a house and a flat was that in a flat 'the owner is quite entitled to masquerade as he pleases'.

Certainly Oliver Hill led his client on quite a dance with his decorations. In the hall they were of grey and black looking glass, with a false perspective in glass rather than in *treillage*. The music room was lined in French walnut and then over-painted by George Sheringham (1884–1937), who specialised in theatrical design and had a long association with Nigel Playfair at the Lyric, Hammersmith. His aim was to create the effect of a modern landscape wallpaper while exploiting the grain of the wood. 'A room of delightful fancy and unreality', Reilly called it.

DEVONSHIRE HOUSE   Below: *The dining room, which was, unusually for the period, part of the main run of rooms. It was decorated by William Kent.*

Right: *The 6th Duke of Devonshire's saloon. He adapted the 2nd Duke's entrance hall in about 1820, and embellished the decoration in the 1840s.*

The dining room was a much weightier matter, to which a black and white photograph cannot do justice: the walls were of honey-coloured Botticino marble with a red Verona marble skirting and framing to the windows; the floor was also in the two colours, and the ceiling of alabaster. The chairs were in silver and green and the lights in the corners of onyx, while the table was veneered in verditer from Rhodesia. Who would create such elaborate and imaginative rooms today?

¶ The most direct way from Devonshire House into the heart of Mayfair is up Berkeley Street, but that is now architecturally boring, and the most rewarding way is by Dover Street, because that takes in first Ely House, which has a most distinguished elevation, designed in 1772 by Sir Robert Taylor for Edmund Keene, the Bishop of that see, and then, further up, in Grafton Street, four out of a group of fourteen houses designed by Sir Robert for the 3rd Duke of Grafton from 1768 onwards. From there it is a short walk by way of Hay Hill into Berkeley Square. However, in order to understand the development of Mayfair it is necessary to go first to Grosvenor Square.

DEVONSHIRE HOUSE   Left: *The saloon ceiling, painted by J. G. Crace in a Baroque Revival style in the mid 1840s.*

Above: *Paintings by Old Masters in the Green Drawing Room. Until the house closed in 1914, the major part of the Devonshire picture collection hung here.*

DEVONSHIRE HOUSE

Mr Albert Levy's drawing room (top) *and dining room* (above), *photographed for* Country Life *in 1927. In the early 1920s, the Duke of Devonshire's town house was replaced by an American-style block of apartments, including one with these extravagant interiors designed by Oliver Hill.*

Right: *Grey and black mirror-glass* treillage *by Oliver Hill in the entrance hall.*

70

FOUR

MAYFAIR

Grosvenor Square has always been the heart of the Grosvenor Estate in Mayfair, and it should be dominated by a statue of either
Sir Richard Grosvenor, the 4th Baronet, or of his mother, Mary Davies, who had brought the 500 acres of what became
Mayfair and Belgravia to the Grosvenor family upon her marriage at the age of twelve in 1677. Sir Richard began to consider developing
this area in the years after he succeeded in 1700, and in 1711 he obtained an Act of Parliament to grant building leases.
Nothing happened, however, until the Treaty of Utrecht in 1713 ended the long European war and unleashed a great burst of building in
London. In 1720 Thomas Barlow, the estate surveyor and a carpenter by trade, laid out the Mayfair Estate with Grosvenor Square as
its central feature, and the following year the first building leases were granted in what is now Davies Street. Only in the summer of 1725
did the *Daily Journal* say: 'There is now building a square called Grosvenor Square which for its largeness and beauty
will far exceed any yet made in and about London.'

Colen Campbell produced a design for a monumental treatment of the east side of the square, but that proved too limiting for would-be tenants. It was just over two hundred years later that the Grosvenor Estate attempted to give the square a uniform treatment, but it has only succeeded in rebuilding the north side between 1933 and 1964.

A number of speculative builders were involved in the original development, the most interesting proving to be Edward Shepherd, who also worked as an architect. He signed his first agreement with Sir Richard in 1723. However, until the Survey of London did research on the Grosvenor Estate in the 1970s, his name was only remembered through Shepherd Market. The finest early interiors on the estate survive in houses built by him.

66 BROOK STREET

Edward Shepherd's first interiors are at 66 Brook Street, now part of the Grosvenor Office, a house that he erected on a site leased in 1725 and sold in 1729 to Sir Nathaniel Curzon, the father of Adam's patron at Kedleston, for whom he had already been building in Curzon Street. But it is not clear whether the interior of the house was complete before 1729, or whether it was fitted up for Sir Nathaniel. There are parallels between the vaulting of the staircase and of the hall of 72 Brook Street, also built by Shepherd, but the vaulted ceiling and the walls of the former are much more richly ornamented.

They are a preparation for the Great Room, one of the most unexpected early Georgian rooms in the West End, being a fusion of Baroque, Gibbsian and Palladian ideas. The confusing synthesis becomes less surprising when it is learned that Shepherd completed Canons for the Duke of Chandos in 1723–25 and built Boreham House, Essex, in 1727–28, probably to Flitcroft's designs. There is a Gibbsian Roman character to the order and entablature, while the overmantel, with its relief and attendant putti and movemente mouldings, recalls the Baroque style of the Italian *stuccatori* with whom Shepherd had worked at Canons, and can also be seen at Hall Barn, Maidenhead, and Barnsley Park, Gloucestershire. This makes it one of the earliest surviving examples of an architectural frame for a glass designed as part of a room. Overall, the room is a reminder that in the late 1720s, Lord Burlington had not yet swept all before him, and William Kent was only just developing his own style of architectural decoration, as can be seen at Kensington Palace.

The *Country Life* photograph taken in 1928 shows the woodwork all stripped and the room bare of furniture, but in fact it is one of the few rooms that recalls those contemporary conversation pieces

66 BROOK STREET Preceding pages (left): *The richly ornamented plasterwork on the main staircase.*
(right): *The Great Room as it was in 1928. The house was built in the late 1720s by Edward Shepherd, a speculative builder and architect.*

Left: *The Great Room, with its Baroque overmantel by one of the Italian stuccatori then at work in London.*

by Charles Philips, with stiff figures in rich clothes posed by or sitting on chairs with exaggeratedly swept backs and impossibly curly legs.

12 NORTH AUDLEY STREET

From the street the Regency stucco and present glazing, which gives the house a particularly dead look, would never suggest to a passer-by that behind lies one of the most intriguing early Georgian houses in Mayfair, with a tripartite gallery that is one of the most dramatic English interiors of the 1730s.

Like the interiors at No. 66, it is a room that grows out of ideas of different origins: for instance, the way the end sections are vaulted and framed by Ionic columns is reminiscent of Campbell's treatment of the King's Room at Compton Place, Eastbourne. Yet Shepherd evidently had an unusual talent for syntheses that defy simple analysis, so it is not surprising that there have been attempts to associate the room with that highly original soldier architect, Sir Edward Lovett Pearce, who worked in Ireland, but could have had a connection with the house's first occupant, Colonel (and much later, in 1766, Field Marshall) Earl Ligonier. He appeared as the first occupant when the street and house were rated for the first time in 1730, paying considerably more than his neighbours then and even more from 1732. Does that point to his building and then almost immediate enlargement of the house?

The way that we see that room today is much influenced by the style of the original *Country Life* photographs taken in 1924 by A. E. Henson, which like so many of the period were intended to make it look as large and lofty as possible. The house had recently been taken by Lord Ivor Spencer-Churchill, the second son of the 9th Duke of Marlborough and Duchess Consuelo, and he had employed Philip Tilden to restore it for him. Lord Ivor was born in 1898, and his acquisition of the house is yet another example of his generation's new enthusiasm for Georgian architecture.

12 NORTH AUDLEY STREET *The Long Room, photographed in 1924 (left), when the house belonged to Lord Ivor Churchill, and in 1962 (above), when it belonged to Christabel, Lady Aberconway. The two views show different approaches to architectural photography, with the first playing up – and falsifying – the scale, and the second conveying the combination of intimacy and complexity in the room.*

By 1962 the thinking about photography had changed, and the higher point of vision of Alex Starkey's photographs gives a much truer idea of the scale: it is really a grand idea in miniature.

At that time, the house belonged to Christabel, Lady Aberconway, to whom it had been left in 1947 by Samuel Courtauld. She had found it for him when he decided to leave Home House after the death of his wife, and it was for him that Rex Whistler designed the limewood urns to go in the niches at the ends of the room.

44 GROSVENOR SQUARE

This house, on the south side of the square, was the last one to remain in single occupation. It was taken by Lord Illingworth in 1928, and it remained the home of his widow until 1966, two years before it was demolished. It was a house of historical associations rather than architectural distinction: it was here that the victory at Waterloo was first announced to the Earl of Liverpool, the Prime Minister, who was dining with the Earl of Harrowby, and where, eight years later, the Cabinet would have been assassinated if the Cato Street Conspiracy had worked.

It was built in about 1727 by Robert Scott, a carpenter, but, unlike Shepherd, he had no special imagination as an architect. He also built in Soho, and the builders of 75 Dean Street, a house with a painted staircase whose demolition was a cause célèbre before and after the First World War, erected the adjoining houses in Grosvenor Square. That may explain the similarity of No. 44's painted staircase to the one in the Dean Street house.

Part of it was uncovered again shortly before the house was demolished. It was remembered that behind the Adam Revival decoration of the first-floor drawing room, done by White Allom for Lord Illingworth in 1930, some old painted decoration was supposed to survive. So the panelling on the west wall was carefully taken down to reveal a painted arcade with contemporary figures looking down over the balustrade, as on Kent's staircase at Kensington Palace. It proved to be the upper part of the west wall of the original staircase. Although a dramatic discovery, it was not enough to save the house, and so it was carefully removed and lent to the Victoria and Albert Museum. Its quality is not very high, but it is a reminder of how many early-eighteenth-century London houses had such painted staircases, with the best surviving painting being the Ricci panels from the staircase at Burlington House, and

44 GROSVENOR SQUARE   Top: *Painted decoration of the 1740s on the walls of the original staircase, which was revealed when the 1930s panelling in the drawing room was taken down.*

Above: *The 1930s decoration of the drawing room. By 1961, No. 44 was the last house in the square in private occupation.*

44 BERKELEY SQUARE   Right: *The first flight of William Kent's staircase of c.1742, photographed in 1962.*

complete but lesser survivors being at Marlborough House, 8 Clifford Street, 11 Bedford Row and 76 Dean Street.

¶ *It is typical of London that the two squares in its principal eighteenth-century residential district should have no formal relationship because of boundaries of private estates. The building of Berkeley Square followed on from that of Grosvenor Square, with small houses on the east side starting to go up in 1741. However, partly because the gardens of Devonshire House prevented building at the south end of the square until after the sale of that house in 1920, the square was never as successful or had such large houses as Grosvenor Square. Horace Walpole moved there from Arlington Street in 1779.*

None of the east-side houses survive and the only early-eighteenth-century section of the square is on the west, with two fine houses, Nos. 44 and 45, standing next to each other.

44 BERKELEY SQUARE

This palazzo-in-miniature is one of the secret wonders of London architecture, but it is also one of the puzzles, because no one has ever been able to explain how it came to be built by an

44 BERKELEY SQUARE

Left: *The superb double staircase at first-floor level, photographed in 1939.*
A masterpiece of monumental treatment on a small scale.

Above: *The ceiling of the staircase showing the three sections of the design,*
photographed in 1962.

44 BERKELEY SQUARE *Kent's cartouches, designed to take busts, on the curved north wall of the staircase.*

unmarried lady-in-waiting to two of the unmarried daughters of King George II, a woman of apparently limited means and un-remarkable looks in her mid forties. How did Lady Isabella Finch, one of the five sons and seven daughters of the 7th Earl of Winchelsea, pay for it – and, also, why did she want such a spec-tacular Great Room? Her mother, Lord Winchelsea's second wife, who died in 1743, was the sole heiress to Viscount Hatton; five of her sisters married well; and two of her brothers had appointments in the Royal Household, which could explain her own minor post, but not a fine house in Berkeley Square.

By 1742, when work on it began, William Kent, her architect, was concentrating on Royal commissions and doing less work for private clients, but on this occasion he was evidently working for someone with whom he was on friendly terms, because when he died in 1748, he left her four busts. Here he drew on his experience of the previous fifteen years to design a masterpiece. This, however, could not be guessed from the exterior, nobly restrained as it is.

The entrance hall takes in the bay to the right of the entrance, but it is deliberately simple so as to give no hint of the drama of the staircase that lies behind it. There Kent curved the north wall to form a semicircle and designed the stairs on an imperial plan, with a central first flight rising northwards that divides and then follows the semicircle before straightening to reach the first-floor landing with its answering screen of Ionic columns, made concave in the centre. Behind that can be seen a simpler stair climbing steeply to the second floor, whose landing forms a canopy for the first floor. High above it, the tripartite ceiling explains how the design is worked out – a glazed apse at the north end lighting the stairs, a central barrel vault, and an inner apse over the second-floor landing. But since the space is so restricted – it measures 27 feet by 16 feet – everything happens so quickly that visitors have their breath taken away, and yet are not given time to work out how their

excitement is created. As Horace Walpole rightly said, it is 'as beautiful a piece of scenery as can be imagined'.

While there are echoes of Kent's early designs for the hall at Holkham, when he envisaged horseshoe stairs in the apse, nowhere else did he attempt to play with space in such a way. Nor are there any precursors in English staircases. However, there are descen-dants, not least in Adam's circular stair at Home House.

On the curved north wall are three characteristically Kentian recesses, designed as ovals, with brackets to take busts, and richly framed with gilded plaster ornament by Robert Dawson that makes them into cartouches inspired by earlier, sixteenth-century Italian ornament prints. The scrolling balustrade made by Benjamin Holmes is enriched with curling feathers that are gilded, a design that was copied later in other places, including the hall at Holkham, long after Kent's death.

Since the staircase is better known in photographs, mostly taken by *Country Life*, than in reality, it is necessary to combine and compare the two sets taken by A. E. Henson in 1939 and by Alex Starkey in 1962, because, as with the gallery at 12 North Audley Street (pages 76 and 77), they are taken with two ideas in mind, the earlier set making it look as monumental as possible and the later one showing Kent's ingenuity in creating his effect on such a small scale.

44 BERKELEY SQUARE Right: *William Kent's Great Room, with an overmantel and pier glass of the 1780s that are probably contemporary with the fillet, as it was in 1939.*

Above: *A detail of the Great Room, showing the unique fillet of gilt ribbon and looking glass that edges the damask hangings.*

The door to the left of the screen on the landing leads into the Great Room, the second great thrill of the house. It fills the whole front of the house on to the square, taking in the attic storey to accommodate the deeply coved ceiling, with its mosaic of panels painted in *grisaille* on grounds of red, blue and green and richly framed in gold. At Houghton, Kent had made great use of *grisaille* painting, but here the richer colours create a smouldering effect similar to that of the even more complex ceiling he designed at the same time for the Great Room at 19 Arlington Street.

How Lady Bel furnished the room is not recorded. Nor are there many accounts of life there. One of the few dates from June 1764, when Horace Walpole wrote: 'We had a funereal loo last night in the great chamber at lady Bel Finch's: the Duke, Princess Emily, and the Duchess of Bedford were there.'

The gilt trophy placed at the head of the pier glass between the windows, the style of the draped valances at the windows, and the unusual big panels of (later) damask inset from the dado rail, the edges of the walls, and the cornice – all suggest a late-eighteenth-century English version of a Louis XVI scheme of decoration, like the White Drawing Room at Houghton. These alterations could date from the time of the 1st Earl of Clermont, a newly created Irish peer, who took the house in 1774 and was still there in 1802. That makes sense: a keen sportsman who won the Derby in 1785, he was a friend of the Prince of Wales and Charles James Fox, while his wife was a friend of Queen Marie Antoinette. However, there are no parallels to the fillet around the damask hangings that is in the form of a gilt ribbon framing ovals of looking glass and twisting around circular jewels of glass, but it must be contemporary with the rest of the late-eighteenth-century work.

These changes tie up with the treatment of the Back Drawing Room and boudoir on the west side of the house, which were also refitted in an more obvious English version of the Louis XVI style that is closer to the work of Henry Holland and often attributed to him.

The 1939 photographs show the house when it was the home of Mr Wyndham Clark, whose family had owned it for sixty years and

44 BERKELEY SQUARE   Left: *English Louis XVI decoration of the 1780s, attributed to Henry Holland.*

45 BERKELEY SQUARE   Above: *The town house of Clive of India, which passed by descent to the Earls of Powis, whose coronet on the lantern and name on the door survived until they left in 1936.*

continued to occupy it until the late 1950s, by which time it was the last private house in the square. It was then acquired by Mr John Aspinall to make into the Clermont Club, which opened in 1962; and being an architectural enthusiast, Mr Aspinall took great trouble over its restoration and adaptation by Philip Jebb and John Fowler.

45 BERKELEY SQUARE

The contrast between the façade of No. 44 and those of Nos. 45 and 46, and even more between the interiors of 44 and 45, mark the difference between the authority and originality of William Kent's work and the more stolid character of the designs of more orthodox Palladian architects, such as Henry Flitcroft and Matthew Brettingham. However, the fact their elevations are in stone should be remarked as an early example in the West End. The lease of the site of No. 45 was granted in 1744 to John Devall, the well-known mason, who assigned it to Henry Flitcroft, who was presumably the architect. Its first occupant was William Kerr, Earl of Ancram, later 4th Marquess of Lothian, from 1750–60, while Lady Darnley was at No. 46 from 1745.

What makes the house more interesting is its association with Lord Clive, who bought it in 1760 when he returned from India as the victor of Plassey, and its long connection with his descendants, the Earls of Powis, who continued to occupy it until 1936. Most unusually, the front door bore a brass plate inscribed 'The Earl of Powis', and so that there should be no doubt that the house belonged to a nobleman, the lantern in the overthrow above the steps used to be ornamented with a coronet. It was to mark the ending of the Powis connection that Christopher Hussey wrote about the house in *Country Life* at the beginning of 1937. He was descended from Clive of India on both sides of his family and looked remarkably like him: his Hussey grandmother was the daughter of the second son of the 1st Earl of Powis, the son of Clive of India who had married the Herbert heiress, and his mother was the daughter of the third son of the 2nd Earl.

Lord Clive employed William Chambers to alter the house for him between 1763 and 1767, and it was to him that the ceilings of the two drawing rooms on the first floor have been attributed, although there is some uncertainty because of early-twentieth-century alterations to the house. The photographs show a number of pictures and pieces of furniture that are now to be seen at Powis

Castle, in Wales. They are a reminder how many families liked to keep some of their finest subject pictures in London, and, in fact, contents that now seem an integral part of country houses only went down to them when the town house was given up, or went backwards and forwards over time. In the Back Drawing Room, for instance, can be seen Bellotto's great *View of Verona*, which is regarded as the key to the Clive pictures at Powis. Similarly, the set of gilt seat furniture now in the Blue Drawing Room at Powis is to be seen in the Front Drawing Room at No. 45.

Clive, like Sir Lawrence Dundas, had made a huge fortune, with a known income of £45,000 a year and he, too, put a good deal of it in to houses and property, including his old home, Styche, in Shropshire, and also buying Walcot in the same county and Claremont, building the present house there.

LANSDOWNE HOUSE

What survives of Lansdowne House is surely one of the most pathetic historic buildings in London. After the First World War, the house was not reopened and stood empty except for the period when it was let to Gordon Selfridge. It lost its unusual setting –

45 BERKELEY SQUARE Left: *The staircase hall of the 1740s. The sober dignity of its treatment in comparison with the excitement of the staircase at No. 44 underlines the difference in the architectural personalities of Henry Flitcroft and William Kent.*

This page (top): *The Front Drawing Room.*
(above): *The Back Drawing Room, with Bellotto's* View of Verona, *now at Powis Castle.*

facing eastwards to enjoy the gardens of Devonshire House – when the Mayfair Hotel began to rise in 1927 on part of the grounds of Devonshire House. The 6th Lord Lansdowne, who succeeded that year, decided the house had no future for the family, and in 1929, he sold it and its collection of marbles. Five years later it was cruelly amputated when Westminster City Council decided to link Berkeley Square to Curzon Street: its front range of rooms was demolished when the façade was set back 40 feet and rebuilt in a distorted form and without its wings. Lansdowne House now stares at the side of a modern block across a modern street.

But possibly it was never a complete success, because of the changes of mind – and means – of its owners. The Earl of Leicester, the builder of Holkham, who died in 1759, planned to build an unusually large house on the site to the design of his protégé, Matthew Brettingham. That scheme was taken over by the Earl of Bute, George III's Prime Minister, who went to his fellow Scot, Robert Adam, for a design. However, when Lord Bute fell from power in 1763, he could not afford to build at Luton Hoo and complete his London house, and so, before it was finished, he sold it to the Earl of Shelburne, (created Marquess of Lansdowne in 1784) who, since 1761, had been considering building a house by Adam at Hyde Park Corner. In 1765 he married Lady Sophia Cartaret and returned to public life, and so he decided to take on Bute's house, but on condition that the shell was completed. At some point the plan was turned round, so that the main entrance front was made to face east. By 1768 several of the main rooms were finished, if not completely furnished, and the Shelburnes were able to move in.

The east elevation as completed consisted of a three-storey main block of seven bays, with a slightly projecting centre piece with an Ionic order supporting a pediment and two-storey flanking wings. The centrally placed entrance hall had a screen of Doric columns through which guests passed to reach the central staircase hall and, beyond that, the painted ante-room with a canted bay on the west front. To the left of the hall was a bigger ante-room with an apsidal inner end, and that led through to what was called the Organ Drawing Room on some plans, and what James Adam referred to in 1765 as 'the Room for Company before dinner'. He explained: 'As one of the suite of Levee rooms it is infinitely better to go first in the ante-room and from there directly into the Room for Company before dinner.'

A door from that drawing room led into the dining room, which filled most of the lower, southern, wing of the house, and so guests came into it through the screen of columns at its west end. The room, as re-erected in the Metropolitan Museum of Art, New York, is slightly different in that the two long walls have been switched round. Also, it lacks its original marbles.

LANSDOWNE HOUSE *The dining room by Robert Adam, apparently photographed for* Country Life *for Arthur Bolton's* The Architecture of Robert and James Adam, *published in 1922.*

Alternatively, the company could pass from the Organ Drawing Room to the Painted Ante-Room and then to the drawing room. The last was intended to lead into the gallery that Adam originally designed for Bute as a music room, and then redesigned as a great tripartite library, with a central section and rotundas at each end.

The complete suite of rooms was still not furnished when Lady Shelburne died in 1771. Lord Shelburne then went off to Italy, where he was inspired by Gaven Hamilton to form a more ambitious collection of antique marbles. That in turn led him to revise Adam's plan for the gallery, and over the next years he considered a series of imaginative schemes. The first, at Hamilton's suggestion, was produced by Panini, who planned to combine sculpture with contemporary pictures. Shelburne then went back to the library idea, and in the late 1780s it was carried out by Joseph Bonomi. It was then altered by George Dance, but again his full design was not completed.

After Lord Lansdowne's death his manuscripts went to the British Museum, but his heir had to sell his pictures, which included Leonardo da Vinci's *Madonna of the Rocks*, now in the National Gallery, and his splendid books. In 1819 the 3rd Marquess got Smirke to complete the gallery for the sculpture, which was then the most important collection in a London house. Gustav Waagen, who made his great survey of British collections in the 1840s and 1850s, wrote: 'The appearance of the grand saloon is particularly striking, it being most richly and tastefully adorned with antique sculptures, some of which are very valuable for size and workmanship. The two ends of the apartment are formed by two large apse-like recesses, which are loftier than the centre of the apartment. In these large spaces antique marble statues, some of them larger than life, are placed at proper distances with a crimson

LANSDOWNE HOUSE Above: *The end of the Sculpture Gallery, finally completed in 1816–19 by Robert Smirke.*

Right: *Robert Adam's Painted Drawing Room. A scheme bedevilled by the client's changes of mind and delays that defeated even Robert Adam, and now looking forlorn in the Philadelphia Museum of Fine Art.*

19 HILL STREET *Rex Whistler's mural at the head of the stairs, painted in 1930–31, when Lutyens altered the staircase for his son-in-law, Captain Euan Wallace, and his daughter, Barbara.*

drapery behind them, from which they are most brilliantly relieved in the evening by a very bright gaslight. This light, too, was so designed that neither the glare nor the heat was troublesome.' However, in fact, it is a rather awkward room with a long dark centre section and a shallow, coved ceiling lying between two more brightly lit, semicircle ends.

Naturally, old photographs of such houses concentrate attention on their design and contents rather than their life, and so their significance for their owners in their political lives tends to get forgotten. Certainly that is so with Lansdowne House, because the 1st, 3rd, 4th and 5th Marquesses held a bewildering succession of offices between 1763 and 1916. The 1st Marquess was both Foreign Secretary and Prime Minister; the 3rd was Chancellor of the Exchequer, Home Secretary and Lord President of the Council three times; the 4th was called to the Lords in his father's lifetime and was Under Secretary for Foreign Affairs; and the 5th Marquess was Governor General of Canada, Viceroy of India, Secretary of State for War and Foreign Secretary.

¶ *Walking up the west side of Berkeley Square, a pair of houses with projecting bays and porches form an unusually formal entrance to Hill Street. It now contains more large eighteenth-century houses than any other street in Mayfair, but although the plot sizes are remarkably wide, those who built on them made as little show as possible with their elevations, which are plain to the point of austerity.*

One of its first occupants was Mrs Montagu, who lived at No. 31. Always a weathercock of fashion, in 1750, she embraced the Chinese style, and so wrote: 'We must all seek the barbarous gout of the Chinese; and fat-headed pagods and shaking mandarin bear the prizes from the finest works of antiquity.' Sixteen years later, she got Robert Adam to alter it, but insisted on his incorporating some chinoiserie motifs. But within a few years, she was bored with the house, and embarked on a new and grander one at the north-west corner of Portman Square.

36 HILL STREET Right: *Mid-eighteenth-century plasterwork and one of a set of eight panels painted by Rex Whistler to fit empty frames on the staircase.*

93

19 HILL STREET

The point of this four-bay house was the mural on the staircase, painted in 1930–31 by the twenty-five-year-old Rex Whistler for Captain Euan Wallace MP and his wife Barbara, the eldest daughter of Sir Edwin Lutyens.

After the First World War, Henry Tonks, head of the Slade School, wanted to revive mural painting and in 1924, he got Rex Whistler, who was in his final year at the Slade, his first commission. After that, Tonks pressed for him to be asked to paint the restaurant at the Tate Gallery in 1927.

Lutyens was also an early admirer of Whistler and wanted him to paint in the Viceroy's House in Delhi. So presumably it was at his suggestion that Whistler painted this staircase, just as, later, he got him the commission to paint the panels for the staircase at No. 36.

It is impossible not to be enchanted by his masque-like landscape, a never-never land with its nostalgia for an eighteenth-

36 HILL STREET *Left: A 1930s ideal of an eighteenth-century country house in its setting, as imagined by Rex Whistler in one of his panels on the staircase.*

Above: The staircase showing the relationship of Whistler's panels to the mid-eighteenth-century plasterwork, photographed in 1939.

century world that had not only vanished but in fact had never existed. Yet, at the same time, when one looks at a photograph of it seventy years later, in a context such as this book, is there not also an uncomfortable feeling of a world that had lost the guts and strength of the age that it yearned for? It seems extraordinary that those who gave Rex Whistler his opportunities made so little impression on the climate of opinion that accepted the destruction of Georgian London.

36 HILL STREET

At No. 36, Rex Whistler's commission was rather different in that it consisted of painting a set of eight pictures, of varying shapes and sizes, to fit into an existing mid-eighteenth-century scheme of plaster panels and drops that was once probably quite common in London. As Laurence Whistler has written in *The Laughter and The Urn*, his life of his brother, 'It was like opening eight windows into one romantic landscape, conceived as flowing on round the room.' The view of the country house is particularly evocative of the houses that were appearing in *Country Life* in the mid 1930s, and brings to mind Sir Alfred Beit looking at the illustrations of Russborough in Ireland and copying the chimney-

piece in the dining room there in his new library at Kensington Palace Gardens (see page 172).

The work was commissioned by Mrs Ernest Porcelli, the daughter of R. S. Sloan of Long Island, New York, who had married her husband in 1927. The panels are no longer there; they were taken out after the Second World War and reassembled at Parbold Hall, Lancashire.

¶ *Hill Street runs into South Audley Street, just to the south of South Street, which has in No. 38 the last big house built in Mayfair. It was built by Lord and Lady Aberconway, in 1919–27, to the design of Wimperis and Simpson with Harold Peto. The walk then heads south past 75 South Audley Street and Audley Square to the site of Chesterfield House.*

75 SOUTH AUDLEY STREET   Left: *The conservatory, as photographed for* The King *in 1902.*

Right: *The ballroom. An 1870s scheme combining panels of eighteenth-century Venetian needlework mounted on velvet, late-eighteenth-century French silk portières, and Louis XV and Louis XVI girandoles.*

75 SOUTH AUDLEY STREET

Some years ago, this house, now the Egyptian Embassy, suddenly became a centre of attention when the National Gallery bought a then unknown Tiepolo ceiling painting of *An Allegory with Venus and Time* that was discovered in the house. Originally painted for Palazzo Contarini in Venice, it had been removed from there, probably in 1855, and then acquired by 1876 by Henri-Louis Bischoffsheim, a member of a European banking family. As with the Rothschilds, members settled in different cities; Henri-Louis, whose wife was Austrian, probably came to London in about 1860, and they bought the South Audley Street house in 1872.

His interiors were swept away in another bout of alteration in the mid 1920s, when the house was given up by his heirs after the death of his widow in 1922, but a set of photographs taken for *The King* in 1902 shows rooms of Rothschildean richness and seriousness. On the ground floor at the back of the house were the ballroom, the Blue Drawing Room and boudoir, subtly different in character from Rothschild rooms and indeed quite different from any known rooms in England. He does not seem to have altered the plan of the unusually large house, originally built in the late 1730s by Edward Shepherd, concentrating instead on fine materials and

75 SOUTH AUDLEY SREET

Left: *The view from the Blue Drawing Room to the ballroom, showing the Bischoffsheims' taste for fine materials – tapestries and silks – in place of boiserie.*

Above: *The Blue Drawing Room, with the Tiepolo ceiling painting of* An Allegory with Venus and Time, *now in the National Gallery, London.*

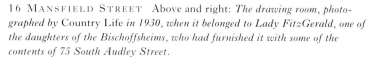

16 MANSFIELD STREET Above and right: *The drawing room, photographed by* Country Life *in 1930, when it belonged to Lady FitzGerald, one of the daughters of the Bischoffsheims, who had furnished it with some of the contents of 75 South Audley Street.*

French furniture, particularly gilt chairs with tapestry covers, but no boiserie. Surely the rooms were designed by a French firm, and one of upholsterers rather than architectural decorators?

The ballroom, for instance, was decorated around a set of panels of what was described in a 1901 inventory as Venetian embroidery mounted on old red velvet. Against the panels are a remarkable number of sconces, twenty in all according to the inventory, six pairs of Louis XVI design and three lots of Louis XV design. There were seven valances of richly embroidered silk, two very large portières of richly embroidered silk, and two of what is called Louis XIII (but possibly a slip for XVI) silk embroidered in silver and gold. It must have been an astonishing room and it is tantalising to have only such sketchy descriptions of it. It is also unusual to see the careful arrangement of stools of different sizes and all raised on a step.

In the Blue Drawing Room, the Tiepolo on the ceiling, described in 1902 as the work of a modern Italian painter, was supported by four small roundels in *grisaille*, and on the walls were huge panels of light blue satin, painted with Classical designs in 'a dull tint', which sounds like eighteenth-century revival on account of the colours and the proportions. The inventory lists four very large old

Gobelins tapestry portières (two on yellow ground and two on pink ground) mounted on a dark-blue velvet and lined with orange-coloured silk, and also the two sets of chairs, but does not describe the wall hangings. Also, there were no less than four chandeliers with fringed stockings.

The boudoir is also a tantalising room, because the wall hangings and portières appear to be of high-quality late-eighteenth-century materials but in different styles, the hangings being Louis XVI in the manner of Philippe de la Salle, and the portières of an equally exceptional, but slightly later, brocaded silk, designed by someone like Pernon. The wall hangings are made up of broad and narrow panels, with the broad panels consisting of three lengths, a central brocaded panel in the manner of Philippe de la Salle bordered with narrow strips in a different technique. The narrow panels are made up in the same way, with a central strip to which the *girandoles* are applied, flanked by a pair of thinner strips that appear to relate to the narrow strips in the broad panels. The overmantel glass and the panels that are made to go with it are faced by a rather differently composed arrangement of painted panels. The whole room is very difficult to analyse, but while it looks as if it was built up out of old materials and old painted panels to create a late-eighteenth-century effect, it seems more likely that the materials were also copies.

75 SOUTH AUDLEY STREET Right: *The boudoir, which appears to have been decorated with high-quality, late-eighteenth-century materials in different styles.*

The Bischoffsheims had two daughters, the Countess of Desart and Lady FitzGerald, the wife of the Knight of Kerry. After the house was sold, Lady FitzGerald moved to 16 Mansfield Street, which was photographed by *Country Life* in 1930, and in one of the rooms there, she reassembled framed panels and other elements from both the Blue Drawing Room and the boudoir together with the Louis XVI chairs from the boudoir. Thus the photographs provide fascinating scope for 'Louis-sleuthing', a more highly developed international sport than chases after English furniture.

CHESTERFIELD HOUSE

Chesterfield House is a dull block of 1930s flats gazing rather blankly down Stanhope Place towards Park Lane and Hyde Park beyond, so it is difficult to appreciate how it owes its name, and its site, to one of the most splendid mid-eighteenth-century houses in

Above: *The entrance hall.* Country Life *photographed the house twice in the time of Lord Lascelles, first for articles in 1922 and then as a record in 1931, when he and his wife, the Princess Royal, gave up the house.*

CHESTERFIELD HOUSE Left: *The great staircase, with its marble stairs and balustrade incorporating Lord Chesterfield's monogram, coronet and Garter.*

Below: *The breakfast room in 1931. This Classical room was on the left of the entrance hall and led into the drawing room.*

London, built by one of the most fascinating men of his time, the 4th Earl of Chesterfield, a politician and diplomat, wit and letter-writer. His house stood on an unusually large plot and was the first large house to face the park. Its front extended almost from Audley Square – Nos. 1 and 2 South Audley Street are built on part of its site – to Curzon Street, and its extensive garden behind filled all the space between Hill Street, the back of Chesterfield Street and Curzon Street.

Chesterfield House has always been tantalisingly famous for its rooms in the French taste, but how did Isaac Ware, who in his *Complete Body of Architecture*, published in 1756 at the start of the Seven Years War, professed a strong antipathy to things French, come to design them for Lord Chesterfield? However, they were but one element in what was arguably the finest Great House completed in London in the 1740s, coming between Devonshire House in the 1730s and Norfolk House, completed in the mid 1750s. Lord Chesterfield's descendants continued to own it until 1870, when it was sold by the 7th Earl, and during that time it was virtually unaltered.

It was then bought by a Mr Magniac, who preserved the main block of the house, but recouped the cost by reducing the width of the plot, so that the colonnades, which had set off the house like extended Ls, were rebuilt as side screens to a smaller forecourt; he also sold off part of the garden. In the 1880s, his successor Lord Burton built extra rooms above Ware's wings containing his great room and library; he also doubled one of Ware's French rooms at the head of the stairs to form a long ballroom extending the full depth of the house; and he added extra ornament to some of Ware's ceilings, following the architect's engraved designs.

Some forty years later Lord Lascelles, the son of the 6th Earl of Harewood and also the heir to his great-uncle, the 2nd Marquess of Clanricarde, who had died in 1916, bought the house shortly before his marriage in 1922 to the Princess Royal, the daughter of King George V and Queen Mary. However, he may have had the idea in his mind for some time because in 1918 he had bought the set of portraits of writers from the library, which had been taken to Bretby in 1870.

It was shortly after Lord Lascelles's purchase of the house that it was illustrated in *Country Life* by H. Avray Tipping, and a second set of unpublished photographs was taken in 1931, presumably when he decided to sell it. Naturally Tipping concentrated on the building and fitting up of the house by Lord Chesterfield, and the unusually full set of photographs is particularly valuable not only as a record of the building, but also of the splendid pictures inherited from Lord Clanricarde, which included purchases, as well as heirlooms, acquired by Lord Lascelles. The latter was advised by Tancred Borenius, who was professor of the history of art at University College, London, from 1922 to 1947 and wrote

CHESTERFIELD HOUSE *The drawing room. The ante-room to the Great Room in the 4th Earl of Chesterfield's day, it was one of the celebrated rooms designed by Isaac Ware in an English version of the French style in the 1740s.*

numerous catalogues of private collections, including *The Catalogue of the Pictures and Drawings at Harewood* in 1936. In an article in *Country Life* on the pictures in 1922, he said that Lord Clanricarde 'took a keen interest in pictures, and for certain schools and period he possessed expert knowledge by no mean order'. To his English and Dutch pictures, Lord Lascelles added other European pictures, particularly of the Venetian High Renaissance, including Cima's *St Jerome in his Solitude*, Titian's *The Death of Actaeon*, now in the National Gallery, Longhi's *Procurate Mocenigo*, which points to the stirring of interest in later Italian painting, and Rubens's *Queen Tomyris with the Head of Cyrus*. Thus the brief Lascelles period in the house proved to be an unexpected Indian summer and the last occasion so far on which a family collection was extended with major historic pictures. It also makes an interesting comparison with what Lord Spencer did more briefly at Spencer House.

However, Lord Lascelles, too, must have found the big house a financial strain, and after he succeeded his father as 7th Earl in 1930 and moved to Harewood, he and the Princess Royal decided in 1931 to give up Chesterfield House.

When it was demolished, in 1934, fittings were scattered and later turned up in a variety of places, ranging from the Bowes Museum at Barnard Castle to the Metropolitan Museum of Art in New York, while the great wrought-iron balustrade of incorporated Cs disappeared until 1965, when it was acquired by the Metropolitan Museum (but never erected). It used to be said that Lord Chesterfield acquired it at the demolition sale at Canons in 1747, but in fact he only bought the marble parts of the staircase and the pillars, which he mentions as 'my Canonical pillars' in a letter of 1748.

Lord Chesterfield was unusual among English men in preferring town life to life in the country. Indeed, he disliked his country seat, Bretby, in Derbyshire, preferring in later life to divide his time between his house in Mayfair and his villa in Blackheath, Ranger's House. 'I love capitals. Everything is best at capitals – the best masters, the best companies, and the best manners. Many other places are worth seeing, but capitals only are worth resideing at.'

However, he was only able to contemplate building a large London house after 1743, when, at the age of forty-eight, he inherited £20,000 from Sarah, Duchess of Marlborough, and his wife inherited from her mother, the Duchess of Kendal, one-time mistress of George I. Two years later he bought the site, and he began to build the house the following year when he returned to London at the conclusion of his Lord Lieutenancy in Ireland.

The scale of the forecourt, with its screens of columns and the exceptional richness of the ironwork in front of the house, made up for the simplicity of the elevation. The front door opened into a single-bay hall, decorated with lavish but typical garlands and drops of Italianate plasterwork, and on the right, three arches in

CHESTERFIELD HOUSE *The library, with Lord Chesterfield's collection of portraits of poets.*

columned screen led through into the staircase hall, with the first floor of a marble-stepped imperial staircase with leading up towards a large Venetian window, before returning in two longer flights to an arched upper screen and landing. It was an unusually grand spatial concept for an English house at that time, quite apart from the elaboration of the balustrade, after a French engraving, incorporating Lord Chesterfield's coronet, monogram and Garter ribbon.

Most of the rooms were in the Palladian tradition, with the French style being confined to the ante-room, to the Great Room – a room to be walked through and so not one for fine pictures – to the music room on the first floor, where heavy decorations and hangings would have deadened the sound, and to the boudoir. However, Chesterfield House was not the only place where Isaac Ware designed decorations in the French taste; he also provided them for Woodcote Park, Surrey, Belvedere in Kent, and for Leinster House in Dublin. But they were never convincing, because he did not use large sheets of looking glass, subject reliefs in carved wood or plaster, or decorative paintings inset in the panelling; moreover, all the proportions remained firmly English, quite different from those in Paris houses.

The change of mood between the hall, the dining room, the ante-room and the Great Room must have been very effective, even if the original idea was modified when the ante-room became the drawing room and the Great Room the dining room, albeit hung with great pictures, so reviving Lord Chesterfield's original idea for the room. Here Lord Lascelles hung Tintoretto's *Portrait of Bendetto Soranzo* in the overmantel, Sebastiano del Piombo's portrait of *A Roman Lady*, and, on the end wall, Titian's *The Death of Actaeon*.

The Great Room was balanced in the south wing by the library, where over the bookcases hung a set of elaborately framed portraits of poets and literary men from Chaucer down to Lord Chesterfield's own day.

CHESTERFIELD HOUSE Above: *The dining room. Originally Lord Chesterfield's Great Room and hung with 'capital pictures', it later became the dining room, and in 1931 it was hung with Italian Renaissance pictures acquired by Lord Lascelles. On the end wall is Titian's* Death of Actaeon.

Right: *The music room on the first floor. In 1922 the room had been shown unfurnished and this unpublished photograph shows it in 1931.*

FIVE

PARK LANE

Walking up Park Lane past the Hilton, Dorchester and Grosvenor House hotels, the blocks of flats and motor showrooms, it is hard
to imagine it as it was eighty to a hundred years ago – a sequence of great mansions interspersed with the Regency bows,
canopies and balconies of smaller houses that seemed to have strayed from the seafront at Brighton to overlook life in Hyde Park.
As Consuelo, Duchess of Marlborough, described it in the 1890s: 'In those days fashionable society was to be seen in
Hyde Park, where in the morning we rode thoroughbred hacks and looked our best in classic riding habits, and where again in the evening,
elaborately decked in ruffles and lace we drove slowly back and forth in stately barouches.' Perhaps this explains why for so long
Park Lane continued to attract those with new fortunes who wished to build large houses, with Leopold de Rothschild at
5 Hamilton Place, Sir Edward Sassoon taking over the house originally built by Barney Barnato, and Alfred Beit and R. W. Hudson
both building new houses.

Of these later houses, only Hudson's survives, the oddly out-of-place, dark-stone, Tudor Revival Stanhope house, designed by W. H. Romaine-Walker in 1899.

It was in the late 1920s that the great houses began to be torn down to make way for hotels intended for New World visitors, and for what Osbert Lancaster, in 1938, called 'pseudo-American cliff dwellings'.

5 HAMILTON PLACE

No collection of old photographs of London interiors would be complete without at least one Rothschild house, and, although none were photographed by *Country Life*, *The King*'s negatives survive for Leopold de Rothschild's house at 5 Hamilton Place, a stone's throw from Londonderry House and around the corner from his father's huge double house, 147 Piccadilly, next door to Apsley House. Now it is the only one to survive, as Les Ambassadeurs, a private club.

Leopold de Rothschild had two brothers: Nathaniel, the 1st Lord Rothschild, who was the main force in the bank in his generation, and Alfred, who seems to have been the most warm-hearted of the brothers. Cecil Roth wrote of him: 'Of men like you/Earth holds but few/An angel – with/A revenue.' All three had been well set up with houses by their father, Nathaniel having Tring and Alfred building Halton on the estate given to him. Leopold came into Ascott, and he also had Gunnersbury and Palace House, Newmarket, as well as Hamilton Place. Although in the bank, his real interests lay in horses – he won the Derby twice, in 1879 and 1904 – and motor cars, being one of the founders of the association that grew into the Royal Automobile Club.

To what extent he inherited the family passion for collecting as opposed to possessions is not clear, and in his choice of architects he seems to have followed his brothers. George Devey, for instance, who altered Ascott for him, had worked for the family since 1867, and William Rogers, who altered the London house in

5 HAMILTON PLACE Preceding pages (left): *The conservatory on the first floor, from a set of photographs taken by* The King *in 1902.*
(right): *The Italian Room, with the dining room beyond. The room was fitted up by Barbetti of Milan.*

Below: *The Louis XV drawing room.*

Right: *A detail of the boiserie, photographed by* Country Life *in 1938.*

5 HAMILTON PLACE

Above: *The richly carved staircase*.

Right: *The boudoir*.

1881, was also involved in the much bigger project of building Halton for Alfred. However, he was also attracted by modern comforts in his houses. Thus No. 5 had one of the first hydraulic lifts, which, according to Frederick Morton, was supposed to be so expensive to operate that it cost more to go from the first floor to the second than to travel by horse cab all through London. And *The King* was impressed by the plumbing: 'In his own bedroom Mr Rothschild has, to use an Americanism, "gone one better" than our neighbours across the Atlantic. He has provided himself with a perfectly fitted-up bath actually at a stone's throw from his bed. What dreams of luxury could surpass this. The other bedrooms, in American fashion, have their bathrooms adjoining.' Unfortunately, the magazine did not photograph the room.

Instead, it concentrated on the varied riches of the interior, the Italian Room or library that was fitted up by Barbetti's studio in Milan, and next to it a dining room that derives from a variety of historical sources without quite making up its mind as to its style.

A richly carved staircase, again of mixed parentage, led up to the two Louis XV drawing rooms, the boudoir and conservatory. Of the latter, the author wrote: 'With the plants and palms standing about in richly coloured vases, and the chairs and tables all in intimate disorder, this makes a delightful picture.' The words surely provide a clue as to why rooms were arranged in that way: it was a conscious attempt to create a picturesque effect and break down the stiffness of richly decorated formal rooms that people found so difficult to live in even then.

19 PARK LANE – LONDONDERRY HOUSE

Londonderry House, on the corner of Park Lane and Hertford Street, although externally unimpressive and only noticeable because of its unusual size, was the last great house in London to fulfil a political and social role. By 1937, as Arthur Oswald wrote in *Country Life*, it had 'become the gallant leader of the old guard, stubbornly maintaining the past traditions of the street in a rear guard action that every year sees the invaders' front advance a little farther'. By 1962, the tower of the Hilton Hotel had been built next door, and Londonderry House was finally was doomed to demolition.

However, when comparing the photographs of it taken in 1902 for *The King*, in the time of the 6th Marquess and his wife (the formidable Lady Theresa Chetwynd Talbot) with those taken for *Country Life* in 1936–37, in the time of the 7th Marquess and his wife, the former Edith Chaplin, who had rearranged it, and reading H. Montgomery Hyde's history of the house published in 1937, it is difficult to decide on its strictly architectural merits. It seems more significant for its atmosphere: it was as if the spirit of Disraeli's only slightly fictionalised account of it as Deloraine

House in *Sybil* had managed to linger on. On the other hand, whereas one can still be swept along by Disraeli's exaggeration, Montgomery Hyde's account now seems uncomfortably hollow.

Ironically, the best features of the house related to the period before the 3rd Marquess of Londonderry bought it in 1822. The original part had been built, or altered, some sixty years earlier by the 6th Earl of Holdernesse, a courtier and diplomat during the reign of George II, who lost office soon after the accession of George III. He had employed James Stuart in the mid 1760s, and when he opened the house in 1767 the result was thought very splendid. Lady Mary Coke wrote: 'The hangings, chairs, and window curtains (of the Great Room) are of three coloured damask, but I think the finest I have ever seen. The glasses are magnificent. Four rooms were open, but not many people; three tables however at which I won four and forty guineas.' Three of Stuart's ceilings survived until 1962, one being similar to those at 15 St James's Square and Spencer House.

The 3rd Marquess, who had succeeded his half-brother, better known when Foreign Secretary as Lord Castlereagh, was able to make the purchase because in 1819 he had married as his second wife the nineteen-year-old Frances Anne Vane Tempest, the daughter of Sir Henry Vane Tempest. She was not only the greatest heiress of her generation, but one of the pushiest women. At the time Lord Londonderry, who had always worked in close harmony with his half-brother, was Ambassador to Vienna and remained there until 1822. His and his wife's ambitions were matched by their fortunes and complemented by her striking looks, set off by staggering jewels, and they called in Benjamin Dean Wyatt and his brother, Philip, to enlarge and transform Holdernesse House to match their view of their new role in the political and social life of London.

Earlier, in 1815–16, Benjamin Wyatt (1755–1855) had designed a great Classical palace for the Duke of Wellington. Then, in the mid

1820s, he began work on what has become Lancaster House for the Duke of York, followed in 1827–28 by the remodelling of Apsley House for the Duke of Wellington, adding on the great Louis Revival Waterloo Gallery. At Holdernesse House in 1825–28, the brothers carried out a similar scheme of opening up the spaces for huge receptions, with a new theatrical staircase and ballroom, and joining the two eighteenth-century drawing rooms to a third in the adjoining house to form what was, in effect, a tripartite saloon. The stairs began as a single flight, then divided at the half-landing and returned in two flights to a balustraded landing, which continued as a gallery round three sides of the well, so that guests could watch those ascending and descending or pass through the screen of columns into the gallery. While the idea was grand, the detailing looks coarse, being possibly altered later, and the effect was never as grand as the staircase hall at Lancaster House when it was finally completed.

Originally sculpture, including several marbles by Canova acquired in Vienna, was important in the gallery, but over the years the Londonderrys developed it into their answer to the Waterloo Chamber at Windsor Castle. In the centre of the north wall hung full-length portraits of three Tsars of Russia, given by the sitters: Alexander I, over the chimneypiece, with Nicholas II to the right, and Alexander II to the left. Alexander I had been a great admirer of Frances Anne, Lady Londonderry, when he met her in Vienna; Nicholas II's portrait was presented to them in 1836; and Alexander II's portrait to the 4th Marquess in 1867. Opposite them were balancing portraits of George IV, the Duke of Wellington and the 3rd Marquess, which Montgomery Hyde describes not wholly convincingly as 'the Csar's three principal contemporaries in England'; while at the end of the room was Lawrence's portrait of Castlereagh in Garter robes. To this set were later added three more full-length portraits, of the 6th Marquess in Garter robes by Sargent, the 7th Marquess by Philpot painted in 1920, and his son, Lord Castlereagh, by de Laszlo painted in 1911. While it would be fascinating now to see these three artists competing with Lawrence, what would people make of the complete complement of sitters? Londonderry House seems to have been the only London house where a family paraded its portraits in this way, rather than hanging them in their country house, in their case Wynyard, their even grander house in Co. Durham.

The rising Disraeli, who was always thrilled to be invited to Londonderry House in Frances Anne's day, left a breathless account of the dinner given after Queen Victoria's coronation: 'Nothing could be more recherché. There were only one hundred and fifty asked and all sat down. Fanny was faithful and asked me, and I figure in the Morning Post accordingly. It was the finest thing of the season. Londonderry's regiment being reviewed, we had the band of the 10th playing on the staircase, the whole of the

LONDONDERRY HOUSE *The ballroom. This was the last Great House in London to fulfil a political and social role.*

said staircase being crowded with the most splendid orange-trees and Cape Jessamines; the Duke of Nemours, Soult, all the "illustrious strangers", the Duke of Wellington and the very flower assembled; it was so magnificent that everybody lost their presence of mind.'

Others found Lady Londonderry's invitations more of an ordeal. Sir Archibald Allison, for instance, found that 'At receptions in her own house her manner was polite and high bred but stately and frigid, such as invariably inspired awe in those who were introduced to her or had occasion to pass her. To such a length did this go that I recollect once in one of her great assemblies at Holdernesse House, as the Marchioness had taken her seat near one of the doors by which the company were intended to go out to bow to them in passing, the whole people the moment they saw her seated in her grandeur turned about and went back the way they came rather than pass through the perilous straits.'

Lord Londonderry died in 1854, and, although Lady Londonderry lived until 1865, the house then entered a relatively quiet period, except that its name was changed to Londonderry House in 1872. Then it sprang to life again in 1884, with the

succession of the 6th Marquess and his wife, who made it a centre of Conservative and anti-Home Rule activity.

Theresa, Lady Londonderry, was a formidable figure, as E. F. Benson records: 'She liked violence and strong colour, and sweeping along with her head in the air, vibrant with vitality. She did not plot or plan or devise, she "went for" life, hammer and tongs, she collared it, and scragged it and rocked it like a highwayman in a tiara, trampling on her enemies as if they had been a bed of nettles – and occasionally getting stung about the ankles in the process – incapable of leniency towards them, or of disloyalty to her friends.'

There is no 1902 photograph of the great dining room prepared for a great occasion, and so the description by Beresford Chancellor in his *Private Palaces* (1908) has to be related to the 1937 *Country Life* photograph, which is in fact most unusual because it suggests

LONDONDERRY HOUSE Below: *The southward view in the drawing room in 1937. One of James Stuart's ceilings of the 1760s can be seen in the centre room.*

Right: *The northward view in the centre part of the drawing room, as photographed by* The King *in 1902.*

how the plate (now mostly in the Brighton Pavilion) was arranged. Of the room, Chancellor wrote: 'it is a dark room, and thus only appropriate for nocturnal festivities; but when the table groans beneath the weight of some of Lord Londonderry's splendid silver-gilt racing trophies ... and the lights of the room are reflected in their dazzling surfaces, then it presents a sense of splendour, as it did when the King of Spain was entertained here, which Lucullus might have envied and Petronius described.'

After the First World War, the 7th Marquess and his wife revived the political traditions of the house, as can be seen from *Country Life*'s frontispiece for 26 November 1932, with the caption: 'As one of the most important political hostesses of the day, Lady Londonderry carries on the great traditions of the past, and gave a brilliant reception at Londonderry House last Monday to meet the Prime Minister.' (See page 17.)

Contrast that with the last days of the house in the late 1950s, when it was hired out for receptions and balls. One of the latter led to an article in *The Express*, 'The Night It Rained Champagne':

DORCHESTER HOUSE Above left: *The entrance front, with Hyde Park beyond. Begun in 1849, it was the last and greatest of the nineteenth-century houses in London.*

Above right: *The staircase and east gallery, looking north.*

Left: *The staircase hall. Robert Holford conceived of his house as a work of art in its own right, and as he told Vulliamy, his architect, this was one of the principal points of view.*

'A debs' coming out party at Londonderry House ended with the police arriving as glasses crashed and champagne flowed in the Park Lane gutter below the first-floor balcony with cigarettes being tossed down to tramps and champagne being poured over the heads of prostitutes.'

DORCHESTER HOUSE

'If the New Zealander, who is to gaze on the deserted site of fallen London in some distant time to come, sees nothing else standing in this neighbourhood, he will certainly find the weather-tinted walls of Dorchester House, erect and faithful.' So wrote *The Builder*, with typically misplaced Victorian confidence, on 28 August 1852, when the still unfinished Dorchester House was noticed for the first time. Yet only seventy-six years later, the house was razed to the ground and its collection of pictures dispersed. This was arguably the greatest loss among houses with collections that London suffered in the first half of this century.

The set of *Country Life* photographs taken in 1928 naturally focuses attention on the building and its interiors and so suggests a secondary role for the collection. In fact, Robert Holford began to collect as soon as he went down from Oxford, and it seems that as his collection developed on historical lines, he conceived of a London house that would display part of it, rather as Lord Ellesmere planned Bridgewater House, begun in 1846. Thus Dorchester House was a deeply serious place dedicated to art and

history rather than to politics and social life, relating to the museum movement of the nineteenth century that was taken up in America by Isabella Stewart Gardner and Henry Clay Frick. As was said in the catalogue of *The Holford Collection*, published in 1927, Robert Holford 'set to work to realize the dream which had taken shape in his head long before of a private house in London which would be in itself a work of art – a natural development of the classical spirit embodied at Genoa and Rome and a visible protest against contemporary Victorian architecture.'

What made it all possible were the profits of his holding in the New River Company, which made him much richer than any of his forebears, who had lived modestly as Gloucestershire squires at Westonbirt. By temperament a dilettante, he took very seriously the responsibilities of a patron of the arts; also, he greatly enjoyed the processes of building and collecting, as well as planting (he began the Westonbirt arboretum in 1829). And no doubt he was

DORCHESTER HOUSE Left: *One of the arches, suggested by Landseer, that linked the saloon to the staircase hall.*

Below: *The Green Drawing Room.*

encouraged by the family of his younger wife, one of whose brothers was Sir Coutts Lindsay, who helped with the decoration of the interior of the house, and whose brother-in-law, the 25th Earl of Crawford, was one of the principal collectors of the time.

As his architect he chose Lewis Vulliamy, the eldest son of B. L. Vulliamy and a former pupil of Smirke. The site he acquired was that of old Dorchester House, which had been altered by Vardy and completed by Chambers for the Damers, Earls of Dorchester, of Milton Abbey in Dorset. It was an irregular plot, but it was prominent, with its two main façades looking down Park Lane towards Decimus Burton's screen and west across Hyde Park. That made the choice of a palazzo form an obvious one, and Vulliamy looked to Rome, to Peruzzi's Villa Farnesina. The design was worked out in 1848–49 and building began in the latter year; the Holfords moved in in 1856, but only four years later was the first of the main rooms completed. The rest of the house, except for the dining room, was finished in 1871.

The porte-cochère led into a dark hall, but ahead could be glimpsed the ante-hall and the Bibiena effect of the great staircase beyond, full of light. To the right lay the porter's room, and on the

left a door led into a vestibule serving Mr Holford's room and a waiting room. Beyond them were two libraries in the west front facing the park.

The whole of the centre of the house was given over to the spectacular grand staircase hall, which could be seen as a highly successful attempt to outshine both those at Stafford House and Londonderry House, and also the central saloon at Bridgewater House. In fact, Holford got the idea as late as 1855, when he saw Palazzo Braschi in Rome, and Vulliamy developed it to make the most of the views through the screens of columns on both floors, which provided ever-changing perspectives as one mounted the stairs. Holford appears to have had an excellent understanding of movement in architecture, but apparently it was Landseer who suggested the cutting through of two great arches so that the saloon should appear beyond the staircase, a dramatic idea that added immeasurably to the Veronese-like splendour of the state rooms.

These consisted of two drawing rooms in the south front, with the saloon to the west – all picture rooms – and the state dining room to the east. The family rooms were on the north side and half the height of the state rooms. The Red Drawing Room had a frieze

DORCHESTER HOUSE Left: *The view from the Green Drawing Room to the Red Drawing Room.*

Top: *The dining room, designed by Alfred Stevens. Its carving was still incomplete after sixteen years of work when Stevens died in 1875, leaving it one of the tragedies of English art and architecture.*

Above: *The end wall of the dining room.*

painted by Coutts Lindsay, and the ceilings of both drawing rooms were painted by an Italian, Anguinetti, whom Holford brought to England in 1861, and who completed the second one by 1863. Work on the saloon proceeded through the 1860s, with painting by a one-legged artist called Morgan and a chimneypiece finally completed by Alfred Stevens in 1869, ten years after he was introduced to Holford and received the commission.

The dining room was surely one of the great tragedies of English art and architecture, for after sixteen years work it still remained unfinished. Stevens had intended that the ceiling should be painted with *The Judgement of Paris* and *The Flight of Aeneas*, and the cove with designs from Geoffrey of Monmouth's chronicle, but none of this was done, and in the end, Coutts Lindsay made designs for the ceiling to be painted as sky with birds. The architectural treatment of the walls was executed as Stevens intended, but again the balance was upset because the painting around the door and in the

panels over the mirrors was not carried out. The only other parts of the room finished when Stevens died in 1875 were the painted doors and the gilt and walnut sideboard. Even the great Michelangelesque figures of the chimneypiece were only finished off by a pupil in 1878.

Of the collection Waagen wrote in 1853: 'Among collections of pictures, that of the Marquess of Hertford unquestionably takes the first place. Next in order may be taken Mr Holford's gallery, in the collection of which a far greater universality of taste has been displayed, consisting as it does not only of the favourite Netherlandish pictures of the seventeenth century, but also of Italian pictures of the golden age of Art.' Thus, as was pointed out in the 1920s publications of the collection, the plates extended from a ninth-century School of Rheims illumination of St Mark to a portrait of Castlereagh by Lawrence.

By the time R. S. Holford died in 1892, the idea of the great London house was on the wane, with Northumberland House already demolished and other houses being sold or let. The collection, part of which was kept at Westonbirt, which he had

BROOK HOUSE *Left and below: Two views of the drawing room, illustrated in* The King *in 1902. The interiors were designed by Wright and Mansfield for the 1st Lord Tweedmouth in the late 1860s.*

rebuilt in the Elizabethan style but never completed internally, remained intact until after the death in 1926 of his son, Sir George Holford. It was then that his executors produced the full catalogue of the collection, prior to sales held in 1927 and 1928.

Considerable attempts were made to save the house through finding another use for it, and Christopher Hussey wrote a passionate plea for it in *Country Life*, illustrated with Gill's photographs. Seventy years later, those articles seem to mark the start of a more militant attitude to preservation of houses both in London and the country, albeit confined to a tiny circle.

¶ *The walk continues up Park Lane past the Grosvenor House hotel, the successor to the Grosvenor family house, now filling the whole block between Mount Street and Upper Grosvenor Street. Beyond that survives a delightful group of houses, stepped at a slight angle and with bows and canted bays. They also suggest the right scale for Park Lane, as can be seen in the way they set off the large, but still comparatively low, Dudley House. That was designed by William Atkinson for the 4th Viscount Dudley and Ward and built in 1827–28 – the last survivor of the great mansions. Just to the north, across Upper Brook Street, is the new Brook House.*

BROOK HOUSE

'There is no need for dwellers in Brook House to dream that they dwell in marble halls. They do dwell in them. They realise what the poet merely imagined.' The house so referred to in *The King* in 1902 is the 'grandfather' of the present one, the 1st Lord Tweedmouth's, which he built to the design of T. H. Wyatt in 1867–69. That was replaced in 1933–35 by the block of flats and penthouse at the top occupied by Lord and Lady Louis Mountbatten, and now that has gone as well.

BROOK HOUSE Above and right: *The 2nd Lady Tweedmouth's boudoir.*

Externally, the Wyatt house was ungainly and never had many admirers, but within it had a run of beautiful rooms on the first floor designed by Wright and Mansfield for the 1st Lord Tweedmouth, and then slightly altered by his son in 1902. Three years later, he sold the house to Sir Ernest Cassel, a great financier and crony of Edward VII, and grandfather of Lady Louis, who inherited it on the death of his sister.

The 1902 illustrations are of particular interest because the 1st Lord Tweedmouth was among the first of his generation to become interested in the Adam period and to collect the finest English furniture of that time, in particular marquetry commodes; he also formed the Wedgwood collection now at the Lady Lever Art Gallery.

Lord Tweedmouth was a banker, a director of Meux's Brewery and the East India Company, an MP, and was closely involved with

the South Kensington Museum, the predecessor of the Victoria and Albert Museum.

In 1856, he finally bought Guisachan, in Aberdeenshire, and he had it redecorated by Wright and Mansfield, who were early specialists in the Adam Revival. Their skill in that direction was recognised at the Paris Exhibition of 1867, where they won an award for the satinwood cabinet inset with Wedgwood plaques that was promptly bought by the Victoria and Albert Museum.

While Guisachan is only known through faded photographs taken in the 1880s, those of Brook House, taken from negatives in good condition, show that the latter had a more Louis XVI character, particularly after the 2nd Lord Tweedmouth installed the large decorative canvases in 1902. The effect recalls the setting that Sir George Sitwell had devised for the conversation picture that he commissioned from Sargent in 1900. However, unlike 75 South Audley Street, it was far from a pure French style, with echoes of James Wyatt and William Chambers, suggesting that English designers were looking towards France. The 2nd Lord Tweedmouth's wife, whose portrait by Waldo Storey appears in the photograph of the boudoir, was a daughter of the 7th Duke of Marlborough and so a sister of Lady Wimborne. *The King* wrote

BROOK HOUSE Left: *The hall and staircase of Lord and Lady Louis Mountbatten's American-style penthouse, constructed at the top of the new Brook House, which in the mid 1930s replaced the Victorian house that had been bought by Lady Louis's grandfather, Sir Ernest Cassel.*

Below: *The three main rooms, facing Hyde Park, which could be opened up for parties or use as a cinema, photographed by* Country Life *in 1939.*

of her in 1902: 'She is one of the few "great ladies" left to act as hostesses at liberal gatherings; but her parties are not by any means exclusively political.'

Until these photographs re-emerged, there did not seem much to regret about the loss of the Tweedmouth house, but at the same time they help to explain why the Mountbattens wanted a simpler, more up-to-date house. But looking back now at their Fifth Avenue penthouse, as photographed by *Country Life* in 1939, it looks rather soulless, except for Rex Whistler's boudoir, which, happily, was taken out at the beginning of the war and survives elsewhere.

On the other hand, the photographs, and, even more, the elaborate plan in the article, graphically illustrate the Americanisation of modern English taste and the new notions of luxury that came with it in the 1930s. The whole concept of the penthouse with its roof garden and upper terrace was taken from New York: in fact, the interiors were by a New York decorator, Mrs Cosden. The style of the main rooms was stripped Classical, with eighteenth-century chimneypieces reused, and they contained fine pictures and objects from Sir Ernest Cassel's collection. But now it seems more remarkable for its plan, which shows it as a social document, with its elaborate offices and staff accommodation.

What seems to have most impressed visitors was the lift, which, according to *Country Life*, was the fastest out of America: 'All sense of speed is lost. Out of it you step into the paved gallery that runs almost the length of the house ... In the middle it widens and rises into a sweeping semicircle staircase.' On the principal floor and facing the park were the dining room, drawing room and morning room, which could be thrown into one for parties or use as a cinema. Beyond the morning room there were two small rooms marked 'Secretary' and 'Cinema Projection', which must have been unique in London.

For the boudoir, on the upper floor, Lady Louis insisted that Rex Whistler should work on canvas so that it could be removed if need be. One of its themes is houses which Lady Louis knew: Broadlands, which she inherited from her father, Lord Mount Temple, over the chimneypiece; Adsdean over the door, balanced by old Brook House. Over Broadlands is a clock against which recline figures of Lord and Lady Louis. It was all done in *grisaille* on a pale greyish-blue ground, and Laurence Whistler described how 'it was as near as mural painting could be brought to book illustration, and being drawn with as much finish – twice over in some areas, for his preliminary drawings are not rough – must have been laborious'.

Lady Louis was all too soon proved to be right, because when the canvases had to be taken out, the original cornice and ceiling in silver had to be left behind and were lost when the building was damaged in 1940. Now, the whole building has been replaced.

BROOK HOUSE *Lady Louis Mountbatten's boudoir, painted by Rex Whistler in* grisaille *on a pale greyish-blue ground. The painting was on canvas, at her insistence, so that it could be removed, and therefore still survives, but without the ceiling.*

SIX

NORTH OF THE PARK

'North of the Park' is a phrase that now sounds very old-fashioned and also rather patronising, hard on those who do not live in Belgravia and are too far away to dine with. But it would have been familiar to all those whose houses come into this section.

The future 2nd Earl of Oxford began to develop his wife's estate in 1717, with Cavendish Square as its centrepiece, but he was too far ahead of demand for it to be a success at the time. It was only in the 1760s that the principal landowner to the west, Henry William Portman, of Orchard Portman and Bryanston, began to develop the estate he had inherited in 1761. Portman Square was the focal point of this, and again, at first, demand was slow. So it was not until 1768 that the houses on the south side began to be occupied. Building on the north side only started in 1774.

PORTMAN HOUSE

Its name records the owners of the estate of which it formed part, rather than its original name of Montagu House, which records its building by Elizabeth Montagu, one of the most remarkable and successful women of her day. Born Elizabeth Robinson in 1720, the elder daughter of wealthy parents, she developed an interest in literature as a child, and, having married Edward Montagu in 1742, she soon established herself as the leading intellectual hostess in London, thanks to her intelligence and charm, and their joint fortunes. From the 1750s they lived in a large house in Hill Street, where she had a famous Chinese dressing room, and gave celebrated literary breakfast parties. 'I never invite idiots to my house' she wrote to Garrick in 1770, and since she was 'handsome, fat, and merry', as Mrs Delany described her, all the most desirable, clever guests came, among them her old friends Lord Lyttelton, Horace Walpole, Dr Johnson, David Garrick, and Sir Joshua Reynolds. When her husband died in 1775, leaving her virtually all his fortune, she decided to move north from Mayfair to Portman Square, where she embarked on the building of a more ambitious house, on a more open site in the still incomplete square.

First she consulted Adam, but he was dismissed for keeping her waiting, and so she turned to James Stuart, who was to cause her problems through delays caused by his drinking. Also, she was building out of income. In 1780 Mrs Montagu could write: 'I am more and more in love with my new House. When a fog obscures Hill Street there is blue sky and a clear atmosphere in Portman Square, and then for my dwelling it is so convenient and cheerful as a place of retirement, so ample for the devoirs of Society, and so calculated for Assemblies that it will suit all one's humours, and adapt itself to all one's purposes. I congratulate myself on having taken the trouble to build it myself.' And in the December of the following year: 'I hope by the end of the week the wishes of my

PORTMAN HOUSE Preceding pages (left): *The drawing room. One of James Stuart's interiors, decorated for Mrs Montagu in the late 1770s and early 1780s.* (right): *The ballroom, designed by Joseph Bonomi in 1789–90.*

HOME HOUSE Above: *The original Front Parlour, with Cézanne's* L'Homme à la Pipe, *Renoir's* La Seine à Asnières, *and Seurat's* Jeune Femme Poudrant, *photographed in 1932, shortly before Samuel Courtauld gave the house to his newly founded Institute.*

Right: *The dining room, with Manet's* Déjeuner sur l'herbe *over the chimneypiece, flanked by Cézanne's* Les Joueurs de Cartes *and Renoir's portrait of Vollard.*

housemaids, the demands of my cooks, and the accommodations of my Butler, will all be fulfilled, completed and answered, and I assure that they will make a total of no significance.' However, by 1782, she was able to move in, although the Great Room was not complete for another eight or nine years. Joseph Bonomi exhibited a design for it at the Royal Academy in 1782, but his final design of 1789–91 was influenced by the Louis XVI style that appealed to the Prince of Wales at the time. The centre of the ceiling was painted by Rigaud and the chimneypiece was carved by Westmacott, while the *verde antico scagliola* columns were by Bartoli. But what must have made the room so striking were the huge looking glasses, balanced by hangings of white-figured damask and curtains of white satin fringed with gold. Here, for a few years, the Queen of the Blues, as she was known, was able to entertain an even larger company until shortly before her death in 1800.

The house was bombed in 1941.

HOME HOUSE

The second set of *Country Life* photographs of Home House taken in 1931 is well known because it is the best record of one of the finest Robert Adam houses surviving in London, showing it

as a private house for the last time. Thus these photographs are always used in articles and books on Adam as a designer of interiors. However, they are even more valuable as a record of the appearance of the house at the end of Samuel Courtauld's time, when he had made almost all his most significant purchases of nineteenth-century French pictures. Since these were made in the years 1924–29, and he purchased the house in 1927, the arrangement was both a very recent one and to be short-lived. After Mrs Courtauld died in 1931, he did not want to go on living in the house and so he gave the lease to a body of trustees, so that the house could be occupied by the new Institute of Art that he had given to London University a few months earlier. He then added a large part of his collection to the gift.

The *Country Life* articles that accompany the illustrations refer to the pictures, but it is the Adam aspect that was Christopher Hussey's main interest. In many ways it was an unlikely story, because Elizabeth, Countess of Home, who built it, was a rich, childless widow in her late sixties when she embarked on it. No one has been able to explain satisfactorily why she wanted to move from her only recently completed house on the south side of the new square and take the largest plot on the north side.

HOME HOUSE

Left: *Robert Adam's staircase.*

Above: *The top of the stairwell. Recently, it has been discovered that*
when he replaced James Wyatt, Adam had to redesign much of the interior,
including this masterly staircase in which he challenged William Kent
at 44 Berkeley Square.

Born in Jamaica in 1704, she had inherited a large fortune from her father, a West Indian merchant, and after a first marriage that left her a widow in her twenties, she had married in 1742 the 8th Earl of Home, but he left her after a year. That was perhaps not surprising, since William Beckford, who was a neighbour, referred to her as 'her infernal majesty' and the Queen of Hell. But why did she want a house so sophisticated in its decoration and in its plan, with its sequence of semicircles and circles, making it a complicated essay in geometry?

It has only recently been discovered that the house was begun by James Wyatt rather than by Robert Adam, and that Adam was only called in after Wyatt was sacked in 1775, when the shell was complete and some of the decoration done. Indeed, several Wyatt ceilings survive. So Adam was faced with the challenge of reworking the interior and turning the constrictions to advantage. However, because the same craftsmen worked for both architects, no one ever suspected two minds at work, and indeed the discovery has increased one's admiration for Adam as a handler of space and designer of exciting interiors.

As Eileen Harris wrote in the key article in the *Burlington Magazine* in May 1997: 'It is particularly ironic that the ingenious

planning of the interior should in the past have been credited to the freedom afforded by the unusual width of the site. The situation was, in fact, quite the opposite. It was the constraints imposed by the house, already built and partly decorated by Wyatt, and the unique challenge of giving a star performance on his rival's stage, that galvanised Adam's creative genius and brought to an even higher peak than it would have reached had he designed the house from scratch.'

An unusually spacious hall leads through to the circular staircase hall, which was entirely redesigned by Adam, who found a solution in answering the challenge of Kent's staircase at 44 Berkeley Square (see pages 80–81). On the ground floor, the main rooms were the front parlour, a rectangle disguised by its four corner columns of porphyry *scagliola*, and, behind it, the eating room,

HOME HOUSE Below: *The music room. Samuel Courtauld restored the mirror-glass decoration and hung on the end wall Renoir's* La Loge *and over the chimneypiece Manet's* Bords de la Seine à Argenteuil.

Right: *The ballroom. Originally the Second Drawing Room, behind the music room, its decoration is a mixture of genuine work of the 1770s and Adam Revival embellishments. Over the chimneypiece can be seen Cézanne's* Montagne Sainte-Victoire.

with a semicircle at its inner end, reflecting the staircase and apse in the hall. Above the front parlour was the music room, which was brilliantly reshaped by Adam; behind it lies the Second or Great Drawing Room, which was decorated around a pair of full-length portraits by Gainsborough of the Duke of Cumberland, the brother of George III, and his wife, Lady Anne Luttrell, which were placed beneath special cornices with draperies like reduced canopies. Their marriage infuriated the King, and that, followed by the Duke of Gloucester's, led to the passing of the Royal Marriages Act of 1772. Indeed, it has been suggested that it was Lady Home's connection with Lady Anne that led her to build the house to provide a setting for the *mal vu* couple.

After her death in 1784, the house passed through many hands, and so it is remarkable that it was so little damaged. From 1920 to 1926, it was occupied by Lord and Lady Islington – she was one of

the best-known country-house and decoration enthusiasts of her day – and after them came Samuel Courtauld.

The best memoir of Courtauld is Anthony Blunt's in Douglas Cooper's catalogue of *The Courtauld Collection* (1954). Samuel Courtauld, who was born in 1876, went straight from school into the family's silk business, and it was while he was getting a proper grounding in textiles that he first began to look seriously at painting. After he married in 1901, he and his wife went to Rome and Florence, where he discovered Italian Renaissance painting. Later, he began to feel that painting seemed to have died with Turner and Constable and to wonder what was missing from modern painting. Before the First World War, he had grown to enjoy classical Picassos, but an exhibition in London of Fauvist painting was a discouragement to him, and he was only brought round to nineteenth-century French painting when he saw Hugh Lane's pictures exhibited at the Tate Gallery in 1917. His final conversion took place at the Burlington Fine Arts Club exhibition in 1922, when he saw Cézanne's *Provençal Landscape*, which Miss Gwendoline Davies had bought in Paris in 1918; the painting is now in the National Museum of Wales.

HOME HOUSE Left: *A bathroom designed for Samuel Courtauld.*

11 MONTAGUE PLACE Below: *The drawing room of Edward Knoblock, who was one of the pioneers of the Regency Revival and collectors of monumental Regency furniture, photographed in 1931.*

By then, he had transformed the family business through developing the manufacture of rayon silk during the First World War, and so amassed his own fortune. This in turn enabled him to establish a fund of £50,000, the income from which could be used to buy nineteenth-century French pictures for the Tate Gallery, and within a few years, it was able to acquire pictures by Cézanne, Seurat, Renoir, Degas and Van Gogh. It was his desire to establish the recognition of these painters that led him to develop the idea of the Institute that he set up in 1931.

He also began to collect their pictures privately, and within five years he had built up the finest group of them in the British Isles, as can still be seen at Somerset House, where the Courtauld Collection is now housed. In the dining room can be seen Cézanne's *Les Joueurs de Cartes*, bought in 1929, Manet's *Déjeuner sur l'herbe*, bought the previous year, and Renoir's *Portrait de M Ambroise Vollard*, bought in 1927. In the Front Parlour, there are Cézanne's *L'Homme à la Pipe* bought in 1927, Renoir's *La Seine à Asnières*, bought in 1929, and Seurat's *Jeune Femme Poudrant*, bought in 1926. In the music room hangs Renoir's *La Loge*, bought in 1925, and Manet's *Bords de la Seine à Argenteuil*, bought in 1923. It is fortunate that *Country Life* recorded it *in situ*.

Home House continued to be used by the Courtauld Institute until 1989, although the pictures had been removed to the Courtauld Gallery, first in Woburn Square and then in Somerset House. After that it stood empty, waiting for a new occupant to take it on. It has now been carefully restored for use as a private members' club, and for those who do not belong there are at least tantalising glimpses of its glittering rooms from the square.

¶ *From the age of Stuart, Wyatt, Adam and Bonomi, the walk leaps into the twentieth century, to a group of houses that show a surprisingly international approach – American, very English, and American-French – to the late-eighteenth-century and Regency Revivals between the wars, to 11 Montagu Place, 11 Titchfield Terrace, now renamed Prince Albert Road and just to the north of Regent's Park, and then to The Holme in Regent's Park.*

11 MONTAGU PLACE

Edward Knoblock, an American, was one of the pioneers of the Regency Revival, and having been interested in the Empire period when he lived in Paris before the First World War, he then discovered the Regency when he moved to England. He bought well at the famous Thomas Hope sale at The Deepdene in 1917, and by 1921 he had created a complete Regency country house at Beach House, Worthing, which was illustrated in *Country Life* that year. His approach to English rooms combined an innate American seriousness and thoroughness with a French sense of elegance.

11 TITCHFIELD TERRACE *The dining room and drawing room. The house of Lord Gerald Wellesley, who combined a scholarly interest in the Regency period with a promotion of the Regency Revival in his practice as an architect between the wars.*

11 TITCHFIELD TERRACE

Almost certainly Knoblock had an influence on Lord Gerald Wellesley, who was a successful practising architect between the wars. He was also a respected connoisseur of eighteenth-century art and the Regency period, as well as being deeply interested in his ancestor, the Great Duke of Wellington, and in his own rooms at 11 Titchfield Terrace there is plenty of evidence of his serious approach to decoration, particularly in his use of wallpapers and choice of furniture and objects that is similar to Knoblock's. Thus it is interesting to be able to compare his own very strong historicism at home with the lighter, thinner and more modern feeling in the work he did for an unnamed client in a house in a Nash terrace.

THE HOLME, REGENT'S PARK

The Holme is one of the few country houses in London, with its view over the lake to the cupolas of Sussex Place. It was the first and best-sited of all the villas in the park. Nash had originally planned for fifty-six houses, but by 1823 the number had been reduced to eight, and of those only four survive. The site of The Holme was taken by James Burton, one of the principal builders of Nash's Regent Street, and he designed it with the aid of his eighteen-year-old son, Decimus. But at the time, it was not admired, and Nash was forced to admit to the Crown Lands Commissioners that 'it is to be lamented, for the beauty of the Park, that Mr Burton was allowed to build the sort of house he has built'.

The house as it exists today owes a good deal to extensions in 1911 and alterations in 1938–39. The latter were done for the Hon. Mrs Peter Pleydell-Bouverie, a daughter of John Jacob Astor IV –

THE HOLME, REGENT'S PARK Left: *The drawing room designed by Stephane Boudin for Mrs Peter Pleydell-Bouverie in 1938–39.*

Above: *The exterior of the house designed in 1823 by James Burton with his eighteen-year-old son, Decimus, for his own occupation. It was the first and best-sited villa in Regent's Park.*

who was drowned in the *Titanic* – and so a cousin of Nancy, Lady Astor. That explains why she entrusted the alterations of the house to Paul Phipps (1880–1953), who was Lady Astor's brother-in-law (and the father of Joyce Grenfell), as well as being the partner of Oswald Milne.

The main interest of the interior, however, lay in the rooms designed by Stephane Boudin, arguably the most brilliant historicist decorator in Paris in the years before and after the Second World War. He worked for the international rich, including the Duke of Windsor, both as Prince of Wales and in exile, but he was never very interested in the English style. Probably the only place here where his work is visible is at Leeds Castle, in Kent. However, while his brilliance is acknowledged, most people find his decoration overworked for life today, and they ignore his great influence on English decoration, particularly through his training of painters and through John Fowler, who was always a great admirer.

He may have owed part of his extraordinary sense of detail to his father having had a *passementerie* factory. In 1923, he joined the firm of Jensen in Paris, and in their workshops he could have anything made or copied if the original was not available, or even

his clients could not afford it. Jensen also had highly skilled draughtsmen and model-makers, as well as Monsieur Cazes, who did the research for the firm, travelling all over Europe looking for authentic designs that could be reused and adapted. Cazes filled almost 120 great volumes with photographs and his own as well as old drawings and prints all arranged by subject, and these remained in the Rue Royale until recently. Thus nothing historical was beyond Boudin.

Mrs Pleydell-Bouverie (1902–56) was evidently a delightful and gifted woman, but beneath the gaiety was an unhappy personality. The daughter of a disastrous marriage, she herself could never make a success of any of her marriages to a series of attractive men. Indeed, *Country Life* could not keep up with them, because on the first batch of photographs, taken in September 1938 by Thompson, she is called Mrs Field – the job was completed by A. E. Henson in

THE HOLME, REGENT'S PARK Below: *Boudin's dining room, inspired by a room in Würzburg.*

Right: *An uncharacteristic and unpublished* Country Life *photograph showing the reflection of Mrs Pleydell-Bouverie in a mirror-glass screen by Syrie Maugham.*

June 1939 – and in the first article on the garden, published on 28 October 1939, she was described as Mrs James Pleydell-Bouverie. Presumably that error or the outbreak of war led to the hold-up of an article on the interior of The Holme, which only appeared as a scrappy shorter article on 20 April 1940, when her name was correctly given.

Boudin found English proportions difficult, and there is a sense of him trying to give the English Regency drawing room a slightly earlier, Directoire feeling, through careful painting and picking out and making the fashionable, smooth satin curtains with draperies trimmed with fringe and tassels, then seemingly little used in England. The overscale chandelier is English Regency, but the Continental character of the pier tables, day bed and chairs, covered to match the curtains, suggest that they were supplied by Boudin; they could have been old, or at least partly old and partly made up in Jensen's workshops.

In the dining room, as so often with Boudin, he disguised his source for the design, and it is not entirely convincing to see it as a fusion of France and England. It then turned out that the room was based on one in Würzburg, recorded in the albums of designs at Jensen. The English elements are the chairs, although perhaps painted up by Boudin, an English table, and the Battersea enamel urns, which were eagerly collected at that time; but the 'Russian', though probably made-up, chandelier and the strips of looking glass in the pilasters are typical Boudin. By the time the room was photographed again by *Country Life* in 1968, it was reduced to its sad bones and so it had lost much of its point, so bearing out how difficult it is to preserve decorators' rooms.

One photograph that was not used in the article is more like *Vogue* than *Country Life*, with its looking-glass screen by Syrie Maugham reflecting the elegant figure of Mrs Pleydell-Bouverie holding a fan. Always interested in the arts, she collected pictures and supported the ballet, paying for Sadlers Wells' first visit to America before the War, and later she was a friend and supporter of many notable writers, painters and dancers, among them Tennessee Williams, Gore Vidal, Frederick Ashton, Edith and Osbert Sitwell and Aldous Huxley. She died in 1956.

1 BEDFORD SQUARE *Above: The entrance to the house.*
Left: *The entrance and staircase hall designed by Thomas Leverton in 1778.*

1 BEDFORD SQUARE

Between the wars, Bloomsbury suffered from the expansion of London University, which gobbled up buildings, and then came the threat of the expansion of the British Museum. So it is fortunate that Bedford Square, which was built between 1775 and 1786, has survived intact as the finest eighteenth-century square in London. One house in it whose future concerned *Country Life* was 1 Bedford Square, which was designed by Thomas Leverton in 1778 as part of the first phase of building in the square, claiming, according to his own account, that he 'had a principal concern in promoting the finishing of Bedford Square'. According to H. M. Colvin, Leverton designed the interiors of at least four of the houses, Nos. 1, 6, 10 and 13. Born in 1743, he was the son of an Essex builder, but nothing is known about how he was trained before he began to exhibit his own architectural designs at the Royal Academy in 1771. At No. 1, Leverton's patron was Sir Lionel Lyde Bt.

The house has one of the most elegant late-eighteenth-century entrance and staircase halls in London: the front door leads into a rectangular centre section, which is divided into three, with deep barrel-vaulted arches framing a larger central area with a shallow dome; arched openings to left and right lead into two apparent ovals, with the staircase on the left rising from right to left towards the light, and the hall proper on the right, the latter providing access to the large room at the back of the house. Elsewhere, Leverton shows himself to have been an ingenious planner, but here he reveals himself to have been a skilled organiser of space and light. Upstairs, there is a handsome Adamesque drawing room with a ceiling incorporating painted panels in the style of Zucchi.

90 GOWER STREET

Who was the first Englishwoman to have a pretty and comfortable bathroom? Was it Lady Diana Cooper in 1920? The idea still seemed novel in country houses in the 1930s when the Trees moved into Ditchley and took great trouble to make the bathrooms both convenient and attractive rather than the usual spartan experience at the end of a long, chilly walk. Certainly Lady Diana's must have been one of the earliest to be photographed, and it was the most memorable room in the house at that stage – until Rex Whistler painted the drawing room in 1928.

Alfred Duff Cooper had married Lady Diana Manners in 1919, and the following year they took 90 Gower Street, which was in a very different district to her parents' house in Arlington Street. Today it seems extraordinary that on an income of £1300 a year, modest by the standards of most of their friends, they could buy a ninety-year lease at £90 a year for £750, to include decoration and fittings, and pay another £100 a year rent for the first floor of the adjoining house, which they took in to make a bedroom and bathroom for Lady Diana.

In *The Rainbow Comes and Goes*, Lady Diana explains how the latter room came about with the help of her mother, the Duchess of Rutland, who was not only an accomplished artist in her own right, but the sister of Harry Lindsay, who together with his wife Norah supplemented their income by helping their friends with their houses and gardens on a professional basis. 'We took a tracing of a Chinese paper at Belvoir and together on ladders we painted the white trees and birds and cages and butterflies on a pale green ground. It had a marble perspective balustrade and, as at Belvoir, a marbled dado. The bath was hidden in a lidded coffer marbled to match. There was a large sofa, a pretty fireplace and gilded looking-glasses ... All the floors were carpeted white to the walls. I felt like a queen in a fairy story and could not ask for more.'

¶ *From Gower Street to Belgravia may not seem a natural architectural walk, but for the energetic Soho still has a few rewards, such as the early-eighteenth-century houses in Meard Street, the painted staircase at 76 Dean Street, the Rococo shopfront at No. 88, and at 1 Greek Street, on the corner of Soho Square, one of the best mid-eighteenth-century staircases and prettiest Rococo ceilings in London – and which can be visited. Then, in the angle between Piccadilly and Regent Street, there are the surprises of the staircase at 8 Clifford Street and ceilings to be enjoyed after dark in Savile Row and Sackville Street, before heading for Hyde Park Corner and the approach to Belgrave Square.*

1 BEDFORD SQUARE   Left: *Neo-Classical decoration in the dining room.*
90 GOWER STREET   Above: *Lady Diana Cooper's bathroom in 1920, with the Chinese wallpaper painted by her mother, the Duchess of Rutland.*

SEVEN

BELGRAVIA TO KENSINGTON

Until the 1950s, as might be expected, *Country Life* showed little interest in London houses built between the Regency and the 1930s, and so there are disappointingly few photographs of interiors of the post-Waterloo period and those in Belgravia. It is almost as if the magazine took the advice of Lady E(gerton) of T(atton) to a young man recorded by William Mallock: 'There are some evening parties at which it will be enough for him to be merely seen; and, with very few exceptions, you should never be seen at a ball in a two-roomed house – a house, for example, like the houses in Eaton Place.'

However, by combining *Country Life* photographs and those taken for *The King*, the walk can follow the spread of London westwards to Kensington, with its artistic houses of the 1860s to 1880s, and end up at Holland House, the earliest of them all, and also the first London house to be illustrated in the magazine in 1905.

5 BELGRAVE SQUARE

There is an unexpectedly strong sense of escapism and make-believe about the ambitious inter-war interiors in London photographed by *Country Life*, and nowhere was that stronger than at 5 Belgrave Square as it was decorated by Mr Henry and Lady Honor Channon. And although the house was dismantled when the Second World War came, the life for which it was created lives on in *The Diaries of Sir Henry Channon*, published in 1967. Henry Channon was an American who settled in London after the First World War and in 1933 married Lady Honor Guinness, a daughter of the 2nd Earl of Iveagh. As he recorded in his diary on 23 March 1935, they decided to buy the house because 'It is not too grand and is dirt cheap compared with all the other houses we have seen.'

By 17 June, they had called in Stephane Boudin, whom Channon said was considered to be the greatest decorator in the world, and he was coming over to design the dining room 'built like the Amalienburg. It will be a symphony in blue and silver ... cascades of aquamarine. Will it be London's loveliest room or is my flame dead?'. Presumably the idea was Channon's, because, following in the footsteps of the Sitwells and particularly Sacheverall, whose *Southern Baroque Art* had appeared in 1924, he had fallen in love with Bavarian Rococo and written a successful book, *The Ludwigs of Bavaria*, in 1933. Early in July 1935, when Boudin brought over the plans for the room, Channon wrote in his diary: ' I think it is

going to be stupendous. There is to be a small ante room opening into a gallery – orange and silver like the Amalienburg: then another door, and then I hope, stupefaction ...'. At the end of the month, Boudin was back again, and Channon noted: 'It will shimmer in blue and silver, and have an ochre and silver gallery leading to it. It will shock, and perhaps stagger London. And it will cost us over £6000.' To set a seal on its success, King Edward VIII came to the first dinner held in it on 11 June 1936, and afterwards Channon wrote: 'I was sad when it was over, it was the very peak, the summit I suppose.'

But it was all too much for Harold Nicolson: 'Oh my God how rich and powerful Lord Channon has become. There is his house in Belgrave Square next to Prince George, Duke of Kent, and the Duchess of ditto and little Prince Edward. The house is all Regency upstairs with very carefully draped curtains and Madame Recamier sofas and wall-paintings.' The Regency interiors were the work of Lord Gerald Wellesley and his partner, Trenwith Wills, with black and gold paintings by Michael Gibbons in the library and by Rex Whistler over the chimneypiece in the drawing room. The style and arrangement of the furniture in the library represent

5 BELGRAVE SQUARE Preceding pages (left): *The approach to Mr Henry and Lady Honor Channon's new dining room as it was in 1938.*
(right): *The blue and silver dining room, inspired by the Amalienburg in Munich, and designed by Stephane Boudin.*

Above and right: *The dining room.*

an English approach that has hardly dated; only the untrimmed shiny satin curtains with their exaggerated draperies proclaim their time.

¶ *Walking through the creamy stucco of Belgravia and then the warm brick and curly gables of the Cadogan Estate, particularly after dark, when first-floor windows are lit up, thoughts about what interesting interiors* Country Life *failed to feature come to mind. After that, as Knightsbridge gets nearer, the architectural interest diminishes, and having not been waylaid by the domes of Harrods, the hunt is on for the Utrillo-in-London view of the dome of the Oratory along Cheval Place, and for the hole in the wall in Rutland Street that leads to the former lands of Kingston House.*

KINGSTON HOUSE

Kingston House is now a monster block of flats with grinning bay windows looking north on to Hyde Park, which makes it hard to visualise the mid-Georgian country house that used to occupy the site. That was photographed by *Country Life* shortly before it was demolished after the death in December 1936 of the Dowager Countess of Listowel, the widow of the 3rd Earl, whom she had married in 1865. In terms of architectural history it is a mystery building that has probably not attracted much attention since the photographs were taken. It was recorded as a complete house that was even then a very rare survival. According to tradition, it was built by the 2nd Duke of Kingston in about 1770, at the time he married the former Elizabeth Chudleigh, who, after his death in 1773, was found guilty of bigamy by the House of Lords, but got off claiming 'privilege of peerage'. However, the house looks old-fashioned for that date and could have been built by the Duke ten years earlier.

5 BELGRAVE SQUARE   Left: *Regency Revival in the library, designed by Lord Gerald Wellesley and painted by Michael Gibbons.*

Above: *The nursery, with the house on the left inscribed* 'Schule'.

Right: *A corner of the library, showing the 1930s satin drapery curtains.*

In 1821 it was bought, together with its lands that are now covered by Ennismore Gardens and Prince's Gate, by William Hare, Lord Ennismore, soon to be created Earl of Listowel. It was presumably he who added the bows to the house, the porte-cochère and the splendid saloon on the garden side to meet the demands of post-Waterloo society. By the 1930s the saloon was a rare interior in London, with its green *scagliola* columns and pilasters with their opulent capitals and the crimson damask hangings and the richly framed pictures of London.

However, even more remarkable are the bedroom, with its mid-eighteenth-century ceiling that suggests the house predated Elizabeth Chudleigh's time, the big kitchen and larder, which was photographed but not illustrated, and the dress coach drawn out of the coach house. Was it the last private dress coach to be kept in London? Today a few survive in the stables of country houses, together with their silver-mounted harness bearing the family arms and their liveries, but it is forgotten when they were last used. The 7th Earl Spencer remembered his family keeping both a dress coach for four people – he was most particular that it was a 'dress' and not a 'state' vehicle – and a dress chariot for two, which were used on state and very formal occasions such as going to Court, a barouche for semi-state occasions and for driving in the park, and a landau or a brougham for everyday purposes.

Lady Helen Seymour, a daughter of the 1st Duke of Westminster, described her mother going from Grosvenor House

KINGSTON HOUSE

Top: *A country house in town – the north front that faced
Hyde Park until 1937.*

Above: *The dress coach, perhaps the last of its kind to be kept in London.*

KINGSTON HOUSE *The saloon, formed by the 1st Earl of Listowel in the early 1920s.*

to the Palace in the late 1890s: 'It was a great amusement to us children to see our Mother dressed in a low evening gown and jewels in the bright sunlight. She was very shy, and these afternoon affairs were an ordeal to her. She drove to Buckingham Palace in the State Coach with the coachman and footmen in State livery, the coachman wearing a wig and a three cornered hat.'

¶ *It may come as a surprise to find that of all the architects the one most fully represented here is not Robert Adam, but Norman Shaw (1831–1912), who was the most prolific and influential domestic architect of the late nineteenth century. Here there are three houses by him: Lowther Lodge, on the corner of Kensington Gore and Exhibition Road; 180 Queen's Gate; and West House, 118 Campden Hill Road. Sadly, there are no photographs here of 49 Prince's Gate, which he altered for F. R. Leyland, and contained Whistler's Peacock Room, or 170 Queen's Gate, where his Classical interiors look forward to those by Lutyens and Oliver Hill.*

LOWTHER LODGE

This country house in town was Shaw's first house in the area, with plans in existence by May 1872, and the house probably finished by 1875. It was commissioned by William Lowther, a nephew of Lord Lonsdale, a former diplomat and Member of Parliament. In 1853 he had married Charlotte Alice Parke, the only daughter of the 1st Lord Wensleydale, a judge. The latter died in 1868, and, although his widow lived on until 1879, it is conceivable that that encouraged the Lowthers to build such an ambitious and complex house in the Queen Anne style.

It is also quite possible that Mrs Lowther pressed for it, because she was a lady of artistic tastes as well as a hostess. William Mallock wrote of her and her circle: 'Let me turn from the world of balls to a milieu which is less frivolous, and take certain ladies as types of tendencies which then prevailed in it. It will be enough to mention four, whose houses represented society as, in some ways, at its best. I refer to Mrs William Lowther, Lady Marian Alford, Louisa Lady Ashburton (whom I thus group together because their isolated and commanding dwellings stood practically in the same row), and Lady Somers. All these were women of the highest

KINGSTON HOUSE Above: *An eighteenth-century bedroom. It probably dates from the time of the 2nd Duke of Kingston, husband of the notorious Elizabeth Chudleigh.*

Below: *The kitchen – a seldom-recorded feature of a London house.*

LOWTHER LODGE Right: *The boudoir and drawing room, photographed by* The King *in 1902.*

cultivation. They were devoted to art. Mrs Lowther was herself an artist. Mrs Lowther and Lady Ashburton, though thorough women of the world with regard to their mundane company, were remarkable for a grave philanthropy which they sacrificed much to practise. Indeed at some of their entertainments it was not easy to tell where society ended and high thinking began.'

Can her attitude be detected in the plan and decoration of the house as it appeared in about 1902? The front door opened into an outer hall, with an inner hall leading into the end section of the north-facing saloon, and then continuing to provide access to the south-facing drawing room and boudoir. The use of the word saloon is striking, for while it has a ring of an eighteenth-century country house about it, it occurs in certain grand mid-nineteenth-century London houses, such as Bridgewater House and Montagu House, and then in certain country houses, where it became a sitting hall, as at Sandringham. The name was obviously carefully chosen by Shaw and was intended to suggest a great hall in a more social and comfortable form, with the big arch dividing off the end section, which was a screens passage in a pre-Classical house. The room had quite a strong Dutch flavour, with its beamed ceiling and gilt leather or leather paper above the high panelled dado, and its

Dutchness is emphasised by the way the light is filtered through the leaded panes on to the deep, leather-covered embrasures, and the use of the brass chandeliers, which seem to have become almost obligatory. However, if the view of it in Andrew Saint's book on Shaw is compared with that taken in 1902, much of the earlier clarity of arrangement of pictures and furniture had been lost in a jungle of screens, plants and draperies.

The drawing room was much more richly decorated: its walls were hung with damask beneath a deep frieze and the plastered ceiling had a pattern of beams, while the doors were hidden by richly worked portières. The chimneypiece looks as if it is mid eighteenth century.

Since 1912 it has been the headquarters of the Royal Geographical Society, which bought it on the recommendation of its president, Lord Curzon, who happened to hear about its availability at a cricket match from James Lowther, the son of the builder who had recently died.

180 QUEEN'S GATE

No. 180, which Norman Shaw designed in 1883, survived intact in the Makins family ownership with its furniture and decorations and collection of contemporary pictures, until shortly before it was demolished in 1971. Thus it was a very rare survival, and fortunately it was recorded by Christopher Hussey in *Country Life* in 1956. However, Andrew Saint, in his 1976 study of Shaw, wrote more fully about its neighbours, saying that 'it had been a little overpraised because of the fine condition in which it was maintained until shortly before its all-too-recent demolition, and because of the Morris papers and furniture installed by the client H. F. Makins'.

LOWTHER LODGE Above: *The saloon, looking east.*

Right: *The saloon, looking west towards the entrance. Norman Shaw designed it as a great hall, but its name suggests its social use.*

The deep corner site with a garden at the back gave Shaw considerable freedom with the plan. On the ground floor at the front of the house, there was a library, and at the back a dining room that was Classical in style with its cornice and panelling and boldly scrolled chimneypiece. However, the most dramatic feature on the ground floor was the stone screen in the hall that led to the main staircase and also hid the service stair: its handling suggested a remote but undefinable past, and yet at the same time it seems to look forward to the work of Lutyens.

The main stair led up to the upper hall, a delightful country room with plenty of white paint, a picturesque interior bay window with leaded lights borrowing light for the service stair, and Morris's Pomegranate wallpaper running up to the low picture rail that left space above for a deep band of white below the Adamesque frieze.

It led into the drawing room, which filled the front of the house. Here, Shaw created a synthesis of allusions out of ideas drawn from different periods: Jacobean windows and glazing, a seventeenth-century idea of a high panelled dado with a rich pattern above, in this case Morris's St James's Palace wallpaper in blue and gold, a

180 QUEEN'S GATE Left: *Eclectic taste of the 1880s in the drawing room – a seventeenth-century Dutch portrait, Victorian paintings, a late-eighteenth-century painted settee, and William Morris wallpaper.*

Top: *The drawing room filled the front of this house designed by Norman Shaw in 1883.*

Above: *The foot of the staircase.*

plaster ceiling with Adamesque ornament in the frieze and on the bed of the ceiling, but used in an un-Adam way with cross beams, and Shaw's own idea of a *c*.1700 marble bolection chimneypiece.

The furnishings were equally eclectic, with a 'Dutch' brass chandelier, a pair of Renaissance Revival inlaid cabinets and a set of late-eighteenth-century English painted seat furniture of the kind that Rossetti had in his house in Cheyne Walk in the 1860s. However, their arrangement does not look at all historical, but as if the room had been thinned out in the course of this century, a process possibly continued by the *Country Life* photographer.

H. F. Makins was a discerning collector of pictures by his contemporaries, especially Millais, whose *Marianna of the Moated Grange* hung to the right of the chimneypiece. And Shaw's panelling suited the moderate scale of many of his purchases: they could be comfortably hung at eye level but without being distracted by the great spaces above.

12 KENSINGTON PALACE GARDENS

If 180 Queen's Gate represents one kind of new house in Victorian London, Nos. 12 and 15 Kensington Palace Gardens are two built as part of an ambitious scheme of a private road of mansions. Begun in the mid 1840s, they were put up on comparatively narrow plots begun on the site of the former kitchen gardens of Kensington Palace. It was a unique concept in London, almost a metropolitan answer to the 'cottages' at Newport in America, and most suitably nicknamed 'Millionaires' Row'. However, like so many London developments, it got off to a slow start, and its first developer, James Blashfield, went bankrupt in 1847. It only became a success in the early 1850s, and even then was never quite accepted as a place to live by old families loyal to Mayfair.

No. 12 is arguably the finest house and it was designed in 1846 by R. R. Bankes, one of Charles Barry's assistants, as might be guessed from its palazzo form, clearly inspired by the Reform Club in Pall Mall. In 1866 it was altered by Matthew Digby Wyatt, who designed the remarkable Moorish billiard room. However, No. 12 is now remembered as the London house of the 5th Marquess of Cholmondeley and his wife, who bought it in 1920, and which Lady Cholmondeley continued to occupy until 1971.

The principal room was the long drawing room, which filled the entire length of the garden front and was divided into three by screens of columns in the manner of Barry's Coffee Rooms in his Pall Mall clubs. However, some of the original detail was simplified, and the chimneypieces were also replaced to make the room more Georgian. Lady Cholmondeley was much less interested in fashionable interior decoration than her brother, Sir Philip Sassoon, but then she had no need of it since she divided her time between this house and Houghton, Sir Robert Walpole's Great

12 KENSINGTON PALACE GARDENS *The drawing room in 1971. One of the last great private rooms in London, with its Cholmondeley and Sassoon possessions, and its view over Kensington Gardens, it was for over fifty years the home of the Dowager Marchioness of Cholmondeley.*

House in Norfolk. Moreover, she had pictures, furniture and objects inherited from her parents and later from her brother to call on, as well as Cholmondeley possessions, such as the tapestries. Thus, despite the very English form of the room, it expressed her own cosmopolitan background and the exotic streak in her character. Throughout her life she fascinated people through her looks, her intelligence and her gifts as a conversationalist, and artists were particularly drawn to her. She was painted by many artists, including Orpen, Sargent and Lavery.

She used to talk about going to No. 12 in 1920, and how amazed her advisers were that she was moving so far from Mayfair, Bayswater at that time seeming as remote as Fulham or Parsons Green today; but quite apart from the character of the house and its view across to Kensington Gardens to the Palace, it was unfashionable and so seemed a bargain. And she often said that it was she who persuaded the French Ambassador to move there, so

establishing its present character as what Mark Girouard has called a diplomatic ghetto.

15 KENSINGTON PALACE GARDENS

Looking back from the end of the century over the vast changes in our civilisation since 1939, it is very hard to visualise the world of the late 1930s that still had sufficient confidence in the future to carry out major schemes of decoration in London. For instance, 15 Kensington Palace Gardens, acquired by Sir Alfred Beit to provide a setting for the collection he had inherited from his father, Sir Otto, in 1930. His transformation in 1937–38 of the house originally designed by J. T. Knowles was one of the most elaborate of its time and was carried out with the aid of Lord Gerald Wellesley and Trenwith Wills.

The collection of pictures, bronzes and majolica had been started in the 1890s by his uncle Alfred, who went from Hamburg to make a great fortune in South Africa and then settled in London. In his collecting he had the advice of Dr Willem von Bode of the Kaiser Friedrich Museum in Berlin; Dr von Bode also advised Sir Julius Wernher, whose career paralleled Alfred Beit's and formed the collection that was at Luton Hoo from after the Second World War

15 KENSINGTON PALACE GARDENS Above: *The oval dining room in blue and silver, designed to display the set of six Murillos of* The Parable of the Prodigal Son.

Left: *The Rococo Revival library designed for Sir Alfred Beit by Lord Gerald Wellesley and Trenwith Wills in 1937–38.*

until recently. When Alfred Beit died in 1906, he left his collection to his brother, Sir Otto, and during the latter's time it reached its peak with about 150 pictures listed in the catalogue, published in 1913. Von Bode insisted on high quality and he found marvellous pictures with a particularly notable group of Dutch and Flemish pictures headed by Vermeer's *Letter Writer*, a pair of Metsus, and pictures by Jan Steen, Ruysdael, Hobbema and Teniers and remarkable Spanish artists, including Velázquez, as well as the Murillos and Goya that appear here.

Unfortunately, there do not seem to be any photographs showing how the collection was arranged in either Alfred Beit's house in Park Lane, or Otto Beit's house in Belgrave Square, which was decorated in the Louis XV and XVI styles by Mewes and Davies. But by the mid 1930s the faux-Louis style would have seemed unsympathetic to someone of Sir Alfred's taste, and he wanted a freer, mostly English house.

At No. 15 there were four main rooms on the ground floor, a comparatively small drawing room found out of the morning room

in the centre of the garden front. Here, the key picture was Goya's *Portrait of Dona Antonia Zarate*, and the room was painted French grey with white woodwork and the columns marbled pale lilac. The upholstery was in lilac and beige stripes, with elaborately draped and trimmed valances of the same material over curtains of yellow shantung and mauve festoon blinds, and window seats with deep bullion fringe. The colours and upholstery here and throughout the house were done by Sibyl Colefax, who had recently been joined by John Fowler, later to become the leading decorator after the Second World War, and here can be seen early hallmarks of his post-war style. Indeed, it is possible to see architectural decoration giving way to interior decoration as it is understood today, which is largely a matter of colour, pattern and materials. All this looks more subtle than the decoration of the Regency Revival rooms at 5 Belgrave Square and makes an interesting comparison with the detail at The Holme, which suggests that John Fowler was already an admirer of Boudin's work. Also in the room can be seen part of the fine set of English Louis XVI-style furniture bought by Sir Alfred and originally from Willersley Castle in Derbyshire.

Since Sir Alfred was not yet married – he married Clementine Mitford in 1939 a few weeks before the outbreak of war – he preferred to have a large music room, which was formed at one end of the house. It was painted *eau de nil*, with mulberry in the upholstery and the rugs, and there were wax candles in the chandeliers. Over the chimneypiece can be glimpsed Hals's *Lute Player*.

The dining room involved a much more elaborate scheme of architectural decoration, being designed in a carefully studied early-Georgian manner with pilasters, entablature and related architectural frames to take the set of six Murillos of *The Parable of the Prodigal Son*. This was painted pale turquoise and picked out in silver, with red japanned chairs copied from a Giles Grendey design that also appears in the photographs of Brook House. A great deal of thought was given to the lighting of the pictures at night, and so the room was designed as an oval, which enabled them to be evenly spotlit, then evidently a new idea, from a central ceiling rose designed by Rex Whistler as a trophy of arms.

The library was the most fanciful of the rooms, an essay in Bavarian or Austrian Rococo, which greatly appealed to Sir Alfred and was chosen here to set off his recent purchase of Jacques de Lajoue's *A Cabinet of Scientific Curiosities*. But what is so curious is that Sir Alfred had the chimneypiece copied from a *Country Life* photograph of the one in the dining room at Russborough, Ireland, which was published in 1937. At that time, he had no idea that he would one day live there.

15 KENSINGTON PALACE GARDENS Left: *Decoration by Sybil Colefax and John Fowler. Lilac-and-beige-striped valances, yellow shantung curtains and mauve festoon blinds in the drawing room* (above), *and a French wallpaper in an Empire bedroom* (below).

8 PALACE COURT, BAYSWATER Right: *The 'Venetian' arch forming the entrance door to the drawing room. In the early 1890s, each room of Mr and Mrs Percy Macquoid's house was designed and furnished in a different style.*

However, after living in South Africa for a few years in the late 1940s and early 1950s, and thinking of returning to Europe, he happened to see an advertisement announcing the sale of Russborough and so he bought it and took the pictures and bronzes there. And it continues to be the home of Lady Beit. In 1976, Sir Alfred created the first foundation in Ireland for a country house.

8 PALACE COURT, BAYSWATER

The identification of these photographs of Percy Macquoid's house, which was made by David Beevers, is especially satisfactory from *Country Life*'s point of view, because through his articles on furniture from 1911, and his work at the end of his life on the *Dictionary of English Furniture* – a project particularly close to the heart of Edward Hudson – Macquoid was a key figure in the establishment of Hudson's broader aims as a publisher. However,

until these photographs were identified, there was no known record of the house that Macquoid got Ernest George and his old friend and best man, Harold Peto, to build for him in the early 1890s. It was a private museum house, with two knowledgeable people creating a serious dream world that is surely a descendant of Horace Walpole's Strawberry Hill and was to influence a remarkable number of people and attitudes to the restoration, furnishing and preservation of old houses over the next forty or fifty years. Each room represented a different style and reflected the growing collection that he and his wife were making. The contribution of Mrs Macquoid, Theresa Dent, whom he married in 1891, often gets overlooked, but not only did she share his interests, doing much of the research for the *Dictionary* and continuing to work on the second and third volumes after his death in 1925, but it was her money that made the house and the collection possible. And it was Mrs Macquoid who left the collection to Brighton.

Percy Macquoid (1852–1925) was the son of a painter and architect who designed furniture. From 1875 to 1887 he exhibited at the Royal Academy, and then in the 1890s he turned to stage design. That may have encouraged him to study decoration and

8 PALACE COURT, BAYSWATER   Left: The chimneypiece in the drawing room. One of a set of photographs taken for The King *in 1902.*

Above: The magnificent drawing room in the style of François I, photographed in 1902.

8 PALACE COURT, BAYSWATER *The dining room, which was supposed to be eighteenth-century English with its Sheraton and Chippendale chairs and mezzotints and drawings on the wall. The late-eighteenth-century chimneypiece came from a house in Dublin.*

furniture, particularly English work. In this he was not quite alone, because in 1892 Frederick Litchfield, a dealer, published his highly successful *Illustrated History of English Furniture*, and that was followed by books by J. Aldam Heaton and T. A. Strange in 1892 and 1900; and the first exhibition of English furniture and silks was held at the Bethnal Green Museum in 1896. However, the photographic record of it, kept at the Victoria and Albert Museum, shows how little was known at that time, particularly about the eighteenth-century period.

Precisely when Macquoid began to collect furniture is not clear, nor what he started with, but as a young man he used to visit the workshops of Wright and Mansfield, who were among the most skilled decorators of their time. However, looking at the François I drawing room of his house as it was in 1902, it would be hard to guess that he would now be remembered for the four folio volumes

that form his *History of English Furniture* and began to appear in 1904, and which are still useful for their excellent photographic illustrations and colour plates. It was his books more than any others that led to a growth in appreciation of English furniture, matched by an increase in prices and the manufacture of old pieces.

The entrance hall had linenfold panelling gathered from different parts of England, and a Gothic door led into the dining room, which was supposed to be eighteenth-century English – 'the style has been rigorously kept throughout, from the Sheraton and Chippendale chairs to the mezzotints and drawings on the walls'. The late-eighteenth-century chimneypiece came from a Dublin house, but, rather oddly, the table was 'a modern one, but one which has been made of "old tops", and polished in the old-fashioned way. This was by rubbing, for twenty minutes at the time, with a piece of flannel having a weight upon it.'

At the entrance to the drawing room was a Venetian arch, while the drawing room itself was 'a magnificent room of the period of François I' – 'Here, reunited once more, are all the vanished splendours of a bygone age.' However, by no means everything was

8 PALACE COURT, BAYSWATER

Top: *Mrs Macquoid's boudoir. Her husband's collecting and writing were supported both by her fortune and her research for* The Dictionary of English Furniture *(1924–27).*

Above: *Percy Macquoid's studio. He had trained as a painter and then turned to stage design.*

French: it was more loosely Continental Renaissance, with the great Flemish tapestry of Jacob and Leah (now in the Burrell Collection) and a brass chandelier suggesting a room in a city like Antwerp rather than London, the chimneypiece from a palace in Venice, panelling from an old house in Devon, oak stalls from a church in Northern Italy, stained glass from Switzerland and furniture of the period of Henri II. The taste seems to have links with the Robber Baron style in America. But who was influencing whom?

Mrs Macquoid's boudoir and her husband's studio were both illustrated. In the former, there was 'carved walnut panelling from a labourer's cottage at Didcot. Above, on a scarlet ground, Mr Macquoid has painted a frieze, consisting of the coats of arms of the various historical personages in whom he is interested.'

In recent years, with the growth of interest in Edwardian interiors, it has also been discovered how Macquoid helped owners such as Lord Stamford at Dunham Massey and Lord Curzon with

18 STAFFORD TERRACE, KENSINGTON Left: *The dining room, photographed in 1952 for* Country Life, *reflects the eclectic mixture of taste of Linley Sambourne, an artist who lived in the house from 1874 until his death in 1910.*

Above: *Stained glass by Linley Sambourne in the drawing room.*

their houses and made purchases for them, acting as an adviser to Morants, who were long-established upholsterers.

18 STAFFORD TERRACE

It is odd that a middle-class Kensington terrace house of the 1870s should be one of the most remarkable survivals in London. But it has scarcely changed since the death in 1910 of Linley Sambourne, one of the principal artists to work for *Punch* from 1867, who was the first to occupy it when he married in 1874. Architecturally, it is a completely standard house, but internally, he made it a special place through the way that he papered and painted it, set stained glass to his own designs in its windows, furnished and arranged it. He composed the rooms with an eclectic mixture of furniture and objects, so that Continental commodes, chairs in the Hepplewhite and Sheraton styles and Windsor chairs were combined with new pieces and are to be found beneath Regency convex glasses and close-hung drawings by his friends and contemporary photographs, all with big mounts and thin frames, and shelves holding blue and white porcelain.

The house meant a great deal to his descendants, who wished to see it preserved. So, after his death in 1910, his son, who was unmarried, lived there, but a more-than-watchful eye was kept on it by his daughter, Maud, who was married to Leonard Messel, a stockbroker, and lived in Lancaster Gate as well as at Nymans in Sussex. Also a talented artist, she loved the house and maintained it after her brother died, later living in it herself during her widowhood. On her death in 1960, it passed to her daughter, Anne, Countess of Rosse, who in 1957 had held the inaugural meeting of the Victorian Society here. She and Lord Rosse always hoped to secure its future, and after his death in 1979, it passed to Kensington Council as one of the last acts of the National Land Fund. It is now run by the Victorian Society.

The house was first photographed for *Country Life* in 1952 for an article by Christopher Hussey, and it is interesting to compare this piece with what he said about the Victorian period in 1931. Through the Rosses' enthusiasm for it and their delight in giving parties in its atmospheric rooms for their friends, who were encouraged to bring along those who would appreciate the house, it became well known in preservation circles. Lady Rosse, who lived in four houses of very different characters, saw them as theatres of life, so complementing the work of her brother, Oliver Messel, as a stage designer, and consequently she only liked people coming to Stafford Terrace when she felt it was ready for a performance. That involved her creating elaborate arrangements of flowers brought up from Nymans. But if one did happen to go round when the Rosses were on their own, Lady Rosse would invariably be needle or patch in hand, repairing a chair cover or curtain so that she kept the rooms looking as if nothing had changed since her grandfather's time.

WEST HOUSE, CAMPDEN HILL

In the mid 1860s and 1870s a new form of house developed in London: the artist's house. It is a graphic comment on the success of the art world and of painters that they could afford to have houses designed and built to suit their particular needs, with studios and rooms where they could display their tastes and entertain. Indeed, a special house became a mark of artistic success, or at least ambition. They tended to be grouped in certain areas in Hampstead, Chelsea, on Campden Hill, and in the area round Holland House, the first being Val Prinsep's and Frederick Leighton's in Holland Park Road, begun in 1865. The latter and William Burges's house in Melbury Road are now the best known.

Norman Shaw was one architect who specialised in them, and he designed the houses for Luke Fildes and Marcus Stone in Melbury Road and also West House, now 118 Campden Hill Road, in 1877 for his friend George Henry Boughton. Although born in England in 1833, Boughton had been taken to America at the age

18 STAFFORD TERRACE, KENSINGTON *The untouched Victorian drawing room, photographed in 1952. The house, now owned by the Victorian Society, was carefully preserved by Linley Sambourne's descendants and is one of the few that can be visited today.*

WEST HOUSE, CAMPDEN HILL *The drawing room. Designed in 1877 by Norman Shaw for George Henry Boughton, an Anglo-American painter, the interiors were photographed for* The King *in 1902.*

of one and brought up there; then, after a period studying in France, he decided to settle in England in 1862. He became an ARA in 1879, and died in 1905.

In the early 1880s his house was included in a series of articles on houses in the *Queen* by Mrs Haweis, which she republished in an artistic little vellum-bound book called *Beautiful Houses* in 1882. Her description can be compared with a series of photographs taken in 1902 for *The King*. Inevitably, there had been some changes in the interval, but they make her sometimes puzzling remarks about periods and style intelligible. She started by making the fascinating observation that 'Mr Boughton has brought from America a certain elegance of style in living which has not yet become common on this side of the Atlantic; less pose than French taste, more subtle than English'.

Mrs Haweis described the rooms in unusual detail: 'The drawing room, charmingly proportioned and lighted by a deep bay window, wears a soft indescribable bloom which is quite uncommon. The means by which this colouring is attained would be most perilous in less skilful hands. Pink and blue strive, but playfully, together on frieze, walls and carpet. The furniture, black lighted with gold, relieves without ever interfering with this harmony, golden panels, adorned with powerful sketches of Spring and Autumn, shimmer one side, on another greenish and bluish porcelain and Venetian glass echo the key note of the room. The mantelpiece, very prettily designed to enclose in its crannies innumerable cups and vases, is painted in two yellows, like the primrose. That this does not clash with the blue and pink is strange, but true. On either side two fine cabinets of black and gold Oriental lacquer give value to that end of the room, and confirm the various hints of Japan, which appear here and there, in panel or curtain. The lower part of the walls is a warm yellow, and the yellow tones into browner amber on chair-seat and portière. The chairs are chiefly Empire Chippendale, but they are not restrained to discomfort.'

WEST HOUSE, CAMPDEN HILL

The library (top). Above the panelling was a deep band of wallpaper, with an oriental wave pattern which echoes the arrangement of porcelain.
The amber-coloured dining room (above). In the early 1880s, the rooms were admired as an example of American taste.

'Empire Chippendale' had long puzzled me and so made the appearance of the photographs particularly welcome, for here was a particularly good Regency chair of the kind particularly associated with later collectors, like Edward Knoblock, and the Regency Revival in the twentieth century and nothing to do with Chippendale. The Boughtons evidently had an eye for quality in furniture of different dates, for there was also a set of Neo-Classical gilt pedestals placed like sentries in the wide openings between the rooms, but the mixture of periods with the brass chandelier, Hepplewhite settee and Regency convex mirror seems to have been a hallmark of artistic taste of that time.

She continued: 'out of this pretty room opens the next, through hangings of amber and Japanese broidery. This room defines somewhat the pearly tint on the side of green. The wainscot, which runs high, is painted of such a green, or blue, as an infant pea forming in the pod, and is hung with fine etchings. The furniture is covered in Morris chintzes. The windows, painted in softest tints, suggest lilies and long leaves, which are realized in numerous plants, flapping and hissing deliciously in the air. Blinds of pale blue silk soften without excluding the light, and the blue sinks in dark blue on the raven-tiles in the fireplace.'

By 1902 this middle room was called the library, even if there appear to have been few bookcases. Above the panelling was a deep band of wallpaper in an oriental wave pattern that echoes the arrangement of porcelain round the fireplace, and it is interesting to see the prints that are a reminder of Whistler's influence through his revival of etching and in the mezzotint after Reynolds, to the left of the door, that recalls the later craze for English mezzotint portraits.

'Opening again hence, the dining-room is a complete and charming contrast. Amber in general tone, the deep soft colouring of Spanish leather, gold, brass, and old oak combine with matting into a singularly pleasing tone. This warmly coloured room is divided by curtains of the softest red plush broken by grey, embroidered in large flowers, for the pea-coloured, which shines beyond with charming effect.'

Upstairs was 'the most comfortable, if not the most beautiful of painting-rooms. The walls and beams are at present greyish drab in tone, the hue of all others best suited to set off other colours near it, and the colours occur in a profusion of beautiful Oriental rugs and embroideries.'

HOLLAND HOUSE

Holland House was the first great London house to be described in *Country Life* on 17 June 1905, and that was appropriate because, after the demolition of Northumberland House in 1874, it was the oldest Great House in London, albeit originally a country house with an estate of almost 500 acres and several miles from the Court.

WEST HOUSE, CAMPDEN HILL *George Henry Boughton's studio.*

The house was originally built by Sir Walter Cope, who also formed the estate, but it owes its name to his son-in-law Henry Rich, who was created Earl of Holland. The connection with the Foxes, who later became Barons Holland of a separate creation, began in 1746 when Henry Fox went to live there. His wife, with whom he eloped when she was twenty-one and he thirty-nine, was Lady Caroline Lennox, one of the celebrated letter-writing daughters of the 2nd Duke of Richmond. She was created Baroness Holland in her own right a year before her husband, because he was in the Government. After leasing the place for a number of years, he finally bought the house and 200 acres in 1768. The Hollands had three sons: Stephen, who succeeded as 2nd Lord Holland but died in 1774; the celebrated Charles James; and Henry Edward. It was during the time of Henry Richard, 3rd Lord Holland (died 1840) and the 4th Lord (died 1860) that the house had such a rich history, partly through their friendships and those of their wives.

HOLLAND HOUSE *Left and below: The Gilt Room. The Jacobean panelling was painted by Francis Clein in about 1630 and touched up in the 1840s by G. F. Watts.*

Henry Richard met his wife, born Elizabeth Vassall, the daughter of a Jamaica merchant and a New York mother, when they were in Italy in 1794 and she was married to Sir Godfrey Webster. They soon fell in love, but only after a costly divorce could they marry in 1797.

Charles Greville wrote of them later: 'Such is the social despotism of this strange house, which presents an odd mixture of luxury and constraint, of enjoyment physical and intellectual with an alloy of small disagreements. Talleyrand generally comes at ten or eleven o'clock and stays as long as they will let him. Though everybody who goes there finds something to abuse or to ridicule in the mistress of the house, or its ways, all continue to go: all like it more or less: and whenever, by the death of either, it shall come to an end, a vacuum will be made in society which nothing will supply. It is the house of all Europe; the world will suffer by the loss; and it may with truth be said that it will "eclipse the gaity of nations".'

The original early-seventeenth-century character of the house survived in the Gilt Room, which was the centrally placed great chamber with the bay window on the south front. It was

remarkable for its original Jacobean panelling with its system of small panels and pilasters and painted overmantels that was created a generation later for Lord Holland by Francis Clein, a painter from the Baltic who settled in England in about 1625, and worked as a decorative painter at Ham House as well as a designer of tapestry at Mortlake. Since the room was burned in the Second World War, the photographs are particularly tantalising, because, while the painting appears as a unique demonstration of early Caroline court taste, with cartouches bearing Jonesian coronets placed above the door and in the corner, the panels display the crest of the Foxes, and it is known that a good deal of touching up was done in the late 1840s by G. F. Watts, to whom the Hollands had become very attached. Also, it is known that the original ceiling collapsed in the late eighteenth century and was replaced by an antiquarian essay in the Jacobean manner.

Among the other rooms photographed by *Country Life*, the most intriguing is the breakfast room, which had been the original entrance hall until the 4th Lord's restoration and changes in 1847, when a new one was formed and it became the main dining room of the house. At that time the original panelling was removed and it was redecorated in a theatrical version of the rich manner of the 1840s, with large eighteenth-century French tapestries of the *Loves of the Gods* and smaller panels over the chimneypieces, flanked by cloth panels of gold embroidery in relief on a ground of crimson velvet, all against the sensible traditions of English dining rooms, and in one corner stood Nollekens's bust of Charles James Fox, which presided over the room. The Jacobean-looking doors with draperies above them must have been recreations of 1847, because they were made to slide on rollers into the thickness of the walls so as to provide vistas through the house on special occasions, but with the doors in the centres used on an everyday basis.

The Holland period came to an end soon after the death of the 4th Lord Holland in 1860, and in 1873, his widow made the place over to the 5th Earl of Ilchester, the great-grandson of Stephen Fox. It was the 6th Lord Ilchester, the historian of the family, who left such a vivid picture of life in the house in his *Home of the Hollands 1605–1820*, and *Chronicles of Holland House 1820–1900*, published in 1937. And it was he and his wife who gave what proved to be the last ball at Holland House, attended by King George VI and Queen Elizabeth in July 1939. Just over a year later, on the night of 27–28 September 1940, the house was gutted by incendiary bombs.

Macaulay foresaw that happening as long ago as 1841: 'The time is coming when, perhaps, a few old men, the last survivors of our generation, will in vain seek, amidst new streets and squares and railway stations, for the site of that dwelling which was in their youth the favourite resort of wits and beauties, of painters and poets, of scholars, philosophers and statesmen.'

HOLLAND HOUSE   *The breakfast room. Charles James Fox's bust presides over the former entrance hall, decorated in a theatrical and eclectic manner by the 4th Lord Holland in the 1840s.*